# Mother Goose and Friends

## An Alphabet Activity Book

## by Becky Daniel

## illustrated by Cara H. Bradshaw

Meet Jack and Jill, Little Boy Blue,
Old Mother Hubbard, Peter Piper, too.
Sing and dance, cut and paste,
Run and jump, cook and taste.
Join Mother Goose and friends
On a trip from A to Z,
Celebrate these nursery rhymes
And learn your ABCs.

## Teaching & Learning Company

1204 Buchanan St., P.O. Box 10
Carthage, IL 62321

# This book belongs to

_____

Cover by Cara H. Bradshaw

Copyright © 1994, Teaching & Learning Company

ISBN No. 1-57310-000-5

Printing No. 9876543

**Teaching & Learning Company**
**1204 Buchanan St., P.O. Box 10**
**Carthage, IL 62321**

TLC10000 Copyright © Teaching & Learning Company, Carthage, IL 62321

# Table of Contents

**Symbol Key**
Circle Time ........................................ ◯

Craft.................................................. △

Pattern Activity ................................... Ａ

Writing Idea........................................ ◇

Puzzle ............................................... ⬡

Game ................................................ ▢

Recipes ............................................. ◡

Awards............................................... ☆

# Dear Teacher or Parent,

Use the familiar and well-loved rhymes of Mother Goose to introduce your young children to the shapes and sounds of the letters of the alphabet. These Mother Goose rhymes and other selections from the classic poetry of childhood have been carefully selected for their lilting charm and child appeal. The companion activities represent a broad spectrum of tie-ins to the early learning curriculum and offer engaging, child-centered projects.

There is a unit for each letter of the alphabet. These units include appropriate nursery rhymes, circle time activities, crafts, letter patterns with directions for making a mosaic, writing projects, games, puzzles, recipes and awards. The highly motivating activities in *Mother Goose and Friends: An Alphabet Activity Book*, are a perfect balance for teaching the total child: hands (physical), heart (emotional) and head (intellectual).

**Hands:** Special attention is given to physical games that build motor skills. Students cut and paste, sing and dance, jump rope, march and run, move to action songs, and perform other exercises designed to teach the alphabet while strengthening coordination.

**Heart:** The young child's emotional needs are addressed with projects, discussions and games to enhance a positive self-image. Affective activities are provided to stimulate positive self-concepts and good citizenship. Youngsters make collages, write poems, create murals, and draw pictures of themselves and discuss their feelings. Many games are designed so that cooperation is a built-in part of the learning.

**Head:** The cognitive skills of learning the shapes and sounds of the letters of the alphabet are presented in a variety of ways designed to let children experience a high level of achievement. It is said that children learn best when they use all five senses to experience new concepts. In this book, the children are asked to make a mosaic of each uppercase and lowercase letter. As they cut out each letter, they are instructed to **feel** the outline of the letter. Writing ideas include sculpting, carving and molding the letters to insure learning in a tactile way. The rhymes, learning activities and crafts are specially designed to reinforce each letter visually. Children will **see** the letters in different colors and sizes all around them. Rhymes, action songs, plays, games and discussions will reinforce the **sound(s)** of each letter. Finally, quick and easy recipes for classroom snacks, lunches and picnics are included to make **tasting** and **smelling** the alphabet a memorable celebration.

Let Mother Goose and the familiar rhymes that many children have heard since infancy become the bridge from home to school. *Mother Goose and Friends: An Alphabet Activity Book* is the perfect transition from lullabies to learning.

Sincerely,

*Becky*

Becky Daniel

# Helpful Teaching Tips

1. Before you begin each unit, you may want to send home a newsletter announcing which letter the class will be studying. You will find reproducible letters on pages 334-344. However, if these letters do not say exactly what you wish to convey to parents, you may choose to use the ideas found in each letter as a springboard for creating your own newsletter. Whether you use the reproducible letters or create a newsletter of your own, it may be helpful to attach a copy of the appropriate rhymes for the unit so parents can recite the rhymes at home with the children. Making parents aware of which letter you are studying will give them the opportunity to reinforce that letter at home. Each reproducible letter also contains a list of needed supplies. When parents send items, collect them in one location. When you begin the unit you will have the materials you need at your fingertips.

2. It is recommended that children make a letter folder for each unit. Fold an 11" x 17" (27.94 x 43.18 cm) piece of construction paper in half or give each child a manila folder. Staple the rhymes to the inside of the front. Staple the recipes to the inside of the back. After children complete the mosaic for a particular letter, they can attach the letters to the outside front of their letter folder. Awards may be attached to the outside of the back. Children can keep games, flash cards, puzzles and activity sheets inside the folder. Pictures the students draw or cut from magazines for each letter can also be added to the folder. After the unit is completed, students can take their letter folder home and share it with family and friends.

3. When introducing the shape of a letter and its sound(s), write it on the board where everyone can see it. Then practice the rhymes several times. Print the rhymes on the board where everyone can see them or display them on a bulletin board. After the rhymes are memorized, children can "read" them. Seeing the word as a child says it is a good first step in learning to read.

4. Art and music are stressed in many of the activities. Creating simple works of art and singing and dancing will make learning the shapes and sounds of each letter fun and memorable. Since attention spans are quite short for some youngsters, the opportunity to move around and experience learning with their whole body will make it more enjoyable.

5. The writing projects are ways of relating to each letter in a personal way. Carving, molding and sculpting letters will help give students a three-dimensional experience to help them remember the letters.

6. Recipes (many are international) are provided for each letter of the alphabet. Some of the recipes are quite involved. These should be prepared by parents at home and brought to the classroom to be eaten at the culminating celebration. Other recipes are simple and can be prepared by the children in the classroom. Sometimes unique foods such as yogurt, zucchini and coconut are called for in a recipe. Don't let new and unusual foods stop your creativity. My daughter Amy says the only thing she remembers about preschool is snacks. "Every day we had a new and interesting food. We didn't have to eat it all, but we had to take a tiny bite of everything! Some of it was yucky, but some of it was really good."

Stimulating the senses with new flavors will expand learning. Before preparing any of the recipes, please check with your students or their parents regarding any food allergies or dietary restrictions which may prevent them from participating with the rest of the class. Change the recipe if necessary. Remember also to be mindful of the size of some foods (berries, nuts, etc.) and the possible choking hazards to young children.

7. Appreciation of nature is stimulated by discussions about the weather, seasons and animals. As often as possible, take the learning out-of-doors and celebrate the alphabet with Mother Nature as well as Mother Goose.

# Aa

Great A, little A,
Bouncing B!
The cat's in the cupboard,
And can't see me.

Here's A, B, C, D, E,
F and G, and
H, I, J, K, L, M, N, O,
P, Q, R, S, T, U, V, W,
X, Y and Z.

Apple pie, apple pudding
and apple pancake,
All begin with **A**.

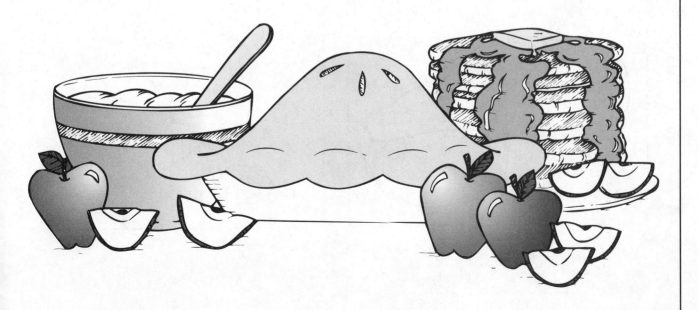

1

# Apple Pie Begins with A

*Apple pie, apple pudding and apple pancake,*
*All begin with **A**.*

**P**ractice the rhyme. Show the picture card for **A** as children say the rhyme. Then play a game to introduce children to other letters of the alphabet. One at a time, show students the picture cards. Some of the foods may need to be discussed. Difficult letters of the alphabet such as **X** and **U** have pictures that may need to be explained. As the leader holds up a picture card, children substitute the food and new letter as they say new verses for the rhyme. Example: If the **B** card is held up, students would say, "Banana pie, banana pudding and banana pancake. All begin with **B**." Use as many or as few cards to introduce new sounds as your group is ready to learn in one lesson. Play the game for short periods of time over an extended number of days.

**Alternative:** Give children their own set of picture cards to color and use as flash cards or to turn into an ABC booklet.

# Cc  carrot

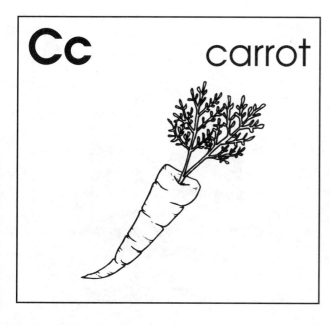

# Dd  doughnut

# Ee  eggs

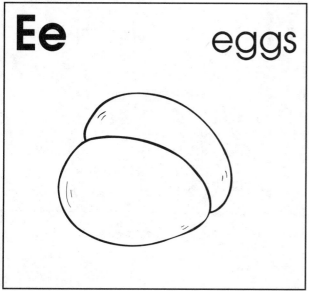

# Ff  fish

# Gg  gum

# Hh  hot dog

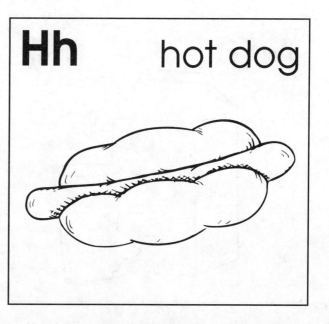

(A)

**Circle Time**

## Ii  ice cream

## Jj  jelly beans

## Kk  ketchup

## Ll  lettuce

## Mm  milk

## Nn  nuts

**Oo** orange

**Pp** pumpkin

**Qq** quiche

**Rr** raisins

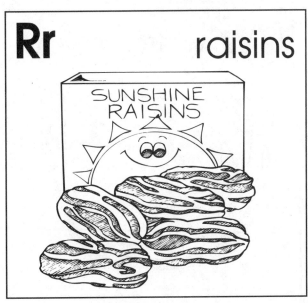

SUNSHINE RAISINS

**Ss** strawberries

**Tt** tomato

**Uu** upside-down cake

**Vv** vanilla wafers

**Ww** watermelon

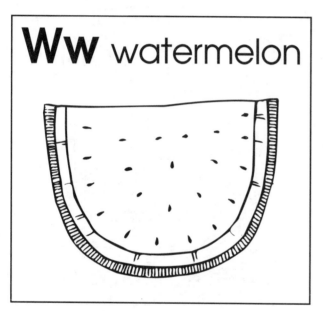

**Xx** hot-cross buns

**Yy** yogurt

**Zz** zucchini

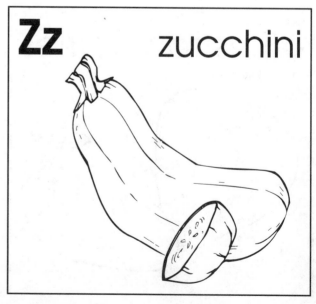

TLC10000 Copyright © Teaching & Learning Company, Carthage, IL 62321

# A Animal Cut-Aparts

**R**eproduce this page and the following four pages and staple together to make a book. Cut along the dotted lines and fold slightly on left margin so each of the sections of each page can be viewed with other sections of other pages.

Staple along this side.

# A Animal Cut-Aparts

Color each body part of each animal.  Use your imagination and as many colors as you'd like!

Staple along this side.

# A Animal Cut-Aparts

Think of names for some of the funny animals you invented. Ask someone to help you make a list of some of the new animals. Example: An animal with an alligator head, ant body and ape feet might be called an aliantape.

Staple along this side.

# A Animal Cut-Aparts

**M**ake a cover for your **A** Animal Cut-Aparts.  Give your book a title and draw pictures of some of the animal combinations on the cover of your book.

Staple along this side.

# A Animal Cut-Aparts

Which of the animal body part combinations do you like best?  Which do you like least?  Do any of them look scary?

Aa

Craft

Staple along this side.

A

# Aqua As

**Pattern Activity**

**Directions:** Use aqua paints (watercolors) to color the uppercase and lower-case **A**s. After the paint dries, glue a few acorns on them. Or draw little anchors, ants, axes or arrows on each one. Cut out and glue them to the front of your **A** folder.

# Sculpting A Snacks

*Apple pie, apple pudding and apple pancake,*
*All begin with **A**.*

**T**o make tasty **A**s, use thawed cookie dough to make A-shaped cookies. Give each child a small handful of dough. Roll into a snake or rope of dough and use to form an uppercase and lowercase **A**. Place on an aluminum foil-lined baking sheet. For students who cannot make the letter shape, draw the shape on the aluminum foil and let the child place his dough along the outline. Before putting cookies in the oven, have students write their initials with a pencil on the aluminum foil for easy cookie sorting later.

**T**hawed bread dough can be used to make individual rolls which students can mark with an uppercase or lowercase **A** before baking.

**A** slice of bread can be decorated by drawing the uppercase or lowercase **A** with apple jelly or apple butter. For easy writing, place jelly or apple butter in a squeeze bottle. Or use the cheese that comes in cans to draw or write **A**s on crackers.

**R**emember, if children can smell **A**s baking and taste the delicious flavor, they are more likely to enjoy the learning!

# As in the Cupboard

The cat's in the cupboard and can't see me. Can you see the cat? What things that begin with the letter **A** can you find in the cupboard?

If you look closely you will find an ant, apple, acorn, alligator, arrow, apron, anchor, angel, airplane, ax and ape.

# A Animal Cages

Cut and paste the animals below in the right sized cage on the next page.

# A Animal Cages

# Alphabet Guessing Game

*Here's A, B, C, D, E, F and G, and*
*H, I, J, K, L, M, N, O, P,*
*Q, R, S, T, U, V, W, X, Y and Z.*
*And here's the child's dad,*
*Who is wise and discerning,*
*And knows this is the fount of learning.*

**Getting Ready:** To play this game, use the cards on pages 2-6. Cut the cards apart and place in a paper bag. One student is chosen to be "It."

**Directions:** "It" draws a card out of the bag. Members of the class ask "It" "yes" or "no" questions about the picture or word on his card.

**Examples:** Is the food on your card red? Is the food on your card a fruit? Does the word on your card begin with a letter that comes before the letter **M**? Students continue asking questions until one player guesses the letter on the card. Give children an opportunity to ask and to answer questions. Then give each student his own copy of the alphabet picture/word cards to color, cut apart and assemble into a booklet or to use as flash cards.

# Appetizing Apples

*Apple pie, apple pudding and apple pancake,*
*All begin with* **A.**

**A**pples are great for teaching the letter **A**. Crunch, munch and chew any of the apple recipes below. Aaaaah, delicious! Each child will need an apple for each appetizing apple recipe. Let each student prepare his apple for the recipes that follow. Begin by washing and peeling apple. Plastic, serrated knives are sharp enough to peel and cut yet safe for little hands. On a cutting board, cut apple into halves, then quarters. Core each quarter. Cut each quarter into four equal slices. (This is a good time to introduce the concept of fractions one half and one quarter.)

## Dried Apples
Colonial America

1. In a small bowl, put juice of half a lemon. Add ¹/₂ cup (120 ml) water. Stir. Soak prepared apple slices (see preparing apple directions above) in lemon water for 2-3 minutes.
2. Thread a needle with a piece of heavy thread approximately 2' (.61 m) long. Pull thread halfway through eye of needle and knot the ends to make a 12" (30.48 cm) piece of double thread. Retie the knot several times so the apples will not slide off the end of the thread.
3. Cut a drinking straw into 15 tiny pieces. Remove apple slices from lemon water and place on paper towels to drain. Alternate apple pieces and straw pieces on thread until all apple slices are strung. Remove needle from thread and tie a loop at top of thread. Mark each child's string of apples with his initials. Hang strings of apples in a warm place to dry for 3-5 days.

## Applesauce
Israel

Wash and peel 8-10 apples. Coarsely chop. Place apples, juice from 1 lemon and 1 thin strip lemon rind in a slow cooker. Add 4 tablespoons (60 ml) sugar and ¹/₄ cup (60 ml) water. Cover and cook on high about an hour until apples are a pulp. Rub through sieve. Add 1 tablespoon (15 ml) butter. Beat well. Cool and chill. To make apple butter, cook apples another hour or until they are as thick as jam. Cool and chill.

# Apple Pies and Cake

## Applesauce Cake

Germany

For a quick applesauce cake, use a prepared spice cake mix. Add 1 cup (240 ml) apple-sauce, 2 eggs and 1/4 cup (60 ml) sour milk. For a spicier cake, add 1 teaspoon (5 ml) nutmeg and 1 tablespoon (15 ml) cinnamon. Optional: Add 1 cup (240 ml) chopped wal-nuts and/or raisins. Bake in a round pan for 1 hour at 375°F (191°C) or until knife inserted in center comes out clean.

## Dutch Apple Pie

Holland

1. Place a ready-made pastry shell in a glass pie pan. Bake for 5 minutes at 450°F (232°C). Remove from oven and let cool.
2. Wash, peel and slice 6 large or 8 small apples and place in a bowl. Drizzle the juice of 1 lemon over the prepared apples. Sprinkle with 2 tablespoons (30 ml) sugar, 1 tablespoon (15 ml) cinnamon and 3 tablespoons (45 ml) flour. Toss.
3. Pour apples in partially baked shell.
4. In a bowl, combine 1 cup (240 ml) sugar, 1 cup (240 ml) flour, 1 tablespoon (15 ml) cinnamon and 1 cup (240 ml) butter. Cut with a knife until you have a crumb consistency. Place topping on apples, piling higher in the middle. Pat down with hands.
5. Place pie in a large brown paper grocery bag. Staple bag closed and bake at 325°F (163°C) for 45 minutes. Remove pie from the bag and bake an additional 15 minutes at 375°F (191°C). Serve warm or cold.

## Apple Pie

United States

1. Have children wash 6 large or 8 small apples. Then using plastic, serrated knives they can peel and core apples.
2. Place one ready-made pie crust in a glass pie dish. Bake crust for 5 minutes at 450°F (232°C). Remove from oven and cool.
3. Place apples in partially baked shell. Sprinkle with 1 tablespoon (15 ml) cinnamon and 2 tablespoons (30 ml) sugar. Carefully place another pie crust on top and seal edges by pressing down with thumb. Cut a big **A** in top crust.
4. Bake one hour at 350°F (177°C). Serve warm or cold.

# Awesome!

_____

knows the shapes of the
uppercase and lowercase **A**.

# Amazing!

You know the sounds the letter **A** makes.

**To:** _____

# ALL RIGHT!

**Y**ou can read these food picture cards.

- [ ] apple
- [ ] banana
- [ ] carrot
- [ ] doughnut
- [ ] eggs
- [ ] fish
- [ ] gum
- [ ] hot dog
- [ ] ice cream
- [ ] jelly beans
- [ ] ketchup
- [ ] lettuce
- [ ] milk

- [ ] nuts
- [ ] orange
- [ ] pumpkin
- [ ] quiche
- [ ] raisins
- [ ] strawberries
- [ ] tomato
- [ ] upside-down cake
- [ ] vanilla wafers
- [ ] watermelon
- [ ] hot-X buns
- [ ] yogurt
- [ ] zucchini

## Absolutely Astounding!

You made a great animal cut-apart book.

**To:** _____

# Bb

Bowwow-wow
Whose dog art thou?
Little Tommy Tucker's dog,
Bowwow-wow.

B was cook Betty
A-baking a pie.
With ten or twelve apples
All piled on high.

Baa, baa, black sheep,
Have you any wool?
Yes sir, yes sir,
Three bags full:
One for the master,
　　　One for the dame,
　　　　But none for the little boy
　　　　Who cries in the lane.

Bowwow, says the dog;
Mew, mew, says the cat;
Grunt, grunt, goes the hog;
And squeak goes the rat.

Tu-whu, says the owl;
Caw, caw, says the crow;
Quack, quack, says the duck;
And what sparrows say you know.

So, with sparrows, and owls,
With rats, and with dogs
With ducks, and with crows,
With cats, and with hogs.

A fine song I have made,
To please you, my dear;
And if it's well sung,
'Twill be charming to hear.

Birds of a feather flock together,
And so will pigs and swine;
Rats and mice will have
　　their choice,
And so will I have mine.

21

# Bowwow-Wow

*Bowwow-wow*
*Whose dog art thou?*
*Little Tommy Tucker's dog,*
*Bowwow-wow.*

**U**se the rhyme to play a getting-acquainted game with the children. Many children do not know each other's middle name. After children are familiar with the rhyme, everyone repeats the first two lines of the rhyme. Then the teacher points to a child. That child says the possessive form of her full name followed by the word *dog* and the last line of the rhyme. Example: John Robert Smith's dog, bowwow-wow. Give everyone a turn to say his full name. (If a child prefers not to use her full name, allow nicknames.)

*Bowwow, says the dog;*
*Mew, mew, says the cat;*
*Grunt, grunt, goes the hog;*
*And squeak goes the rat.*

*Tu-whu, says the owl;*
*Caw,caw, says the crow;*
*Quack, quack, says the duck;*
*And what sparrows say you know.*

**P**lay a guessing game with this rhyme. Children sit in a circle. The first child makes an animal sound. The child on his right says, "Says the (and fills in the correct animal.)" Example: First child says, "Honk, honk." The next child says, "Says the goose." Then that same student makes an animal sound, and the person to the right has to respond with the name of the animal. Repeat around the circle until everyone has a turn.

# Bottled Bs

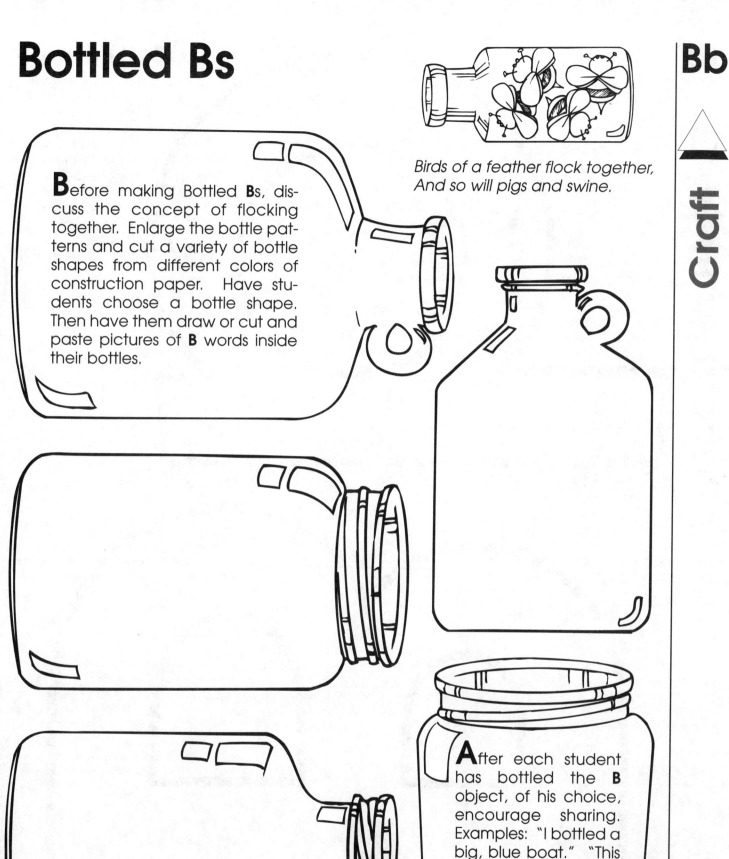

**B**efore making Bottled **B**s, discuss the concept of flocking together. Enlarge the bottle patterns and cut a variety of bottle shapes from different colors of construction paper. Have students choose a bottle shape. Then have them draw or cut and paste pictures of **B** words inside their bottles.

*Birds of a feather flock together,*
*And so will pigs and swine.*

**A**fter each student has bottled the **B** object, of his choice, encourage sharing. Examples: "I bottled a big, blue boat." "This is my bottle of bees." "My bottle is full of a bunny."

**Pattern Activity**

# Beautiful Bs

**Directions:** Make the uppercase and lowercase **B**s beautiful. Color them brown, blue or black. Draw on designs. Decorate them with beans, beads or buttons. When dry, cut them out. Glue them to the cover of your **B** folder.

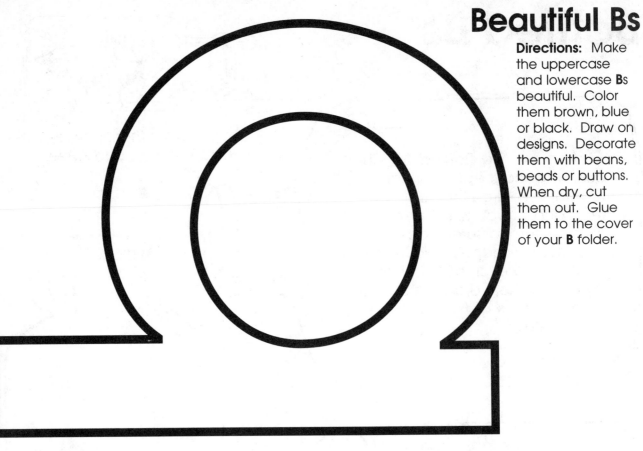

TLC10000 Copyright © Teaching & Learning Company, Carthage, IL 62321

# What's in the Blue Bag?

**R**eproduce the bag below on blue construction paper and provide one for each student. Students cut and paste or print things that begin with **B** in their bags. Who can think of the most **B** things? Who can fill the bag the fullest? When students have completed the project, allow time for sharing. Who thought of something that no one else thought of? What **B** object was found most often in the bags? What was the biggest **B** object in a bag? Smallest? Bluest? Brightest? Best?

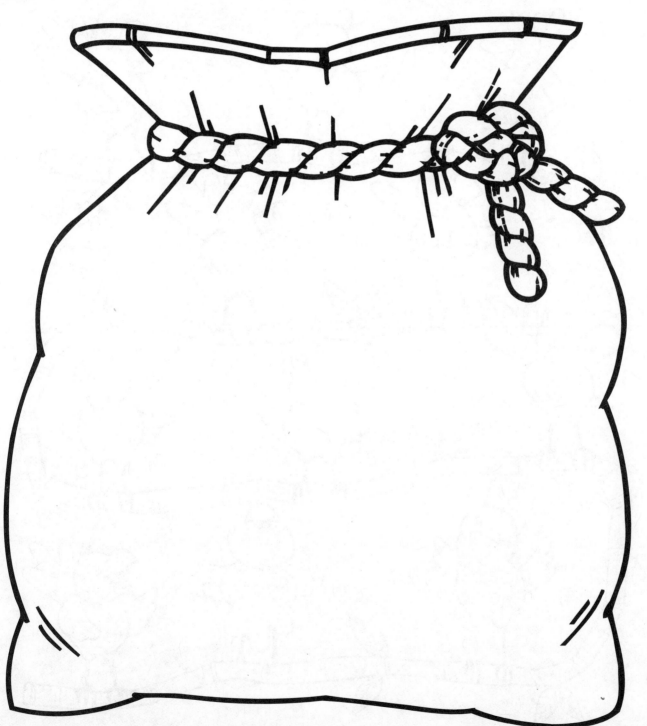

# Birds of a Feather

*Birds of a feather flock together,*
*And so will pigs and swine;*
*Rats and mice will have their choice,*
*And so will I have mine.*

Color the matching birds the same color.

# Basket of B Foods

Color and cut out some of your favorite foods that begin with the letter **B** on the next page. Paste them in the basket below. Color the basket your favorite color. Make it beautiful!

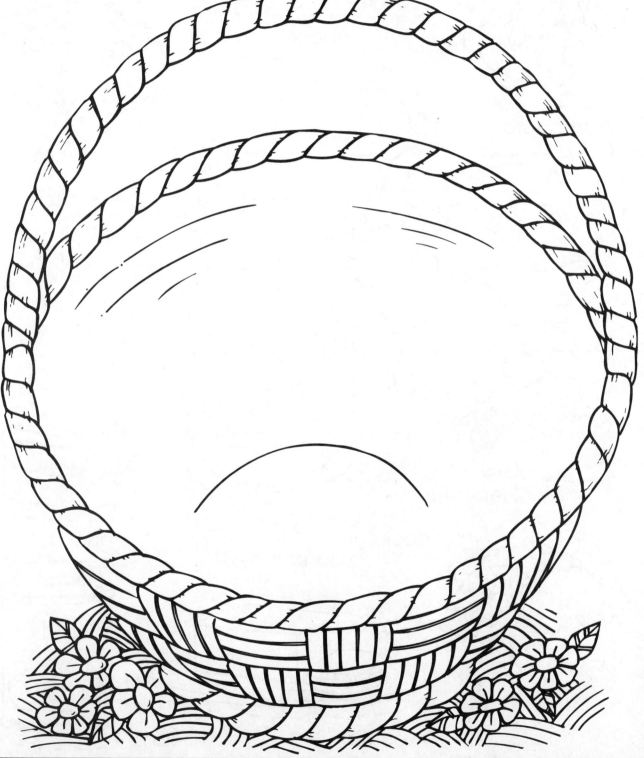

# Basket of B Foods

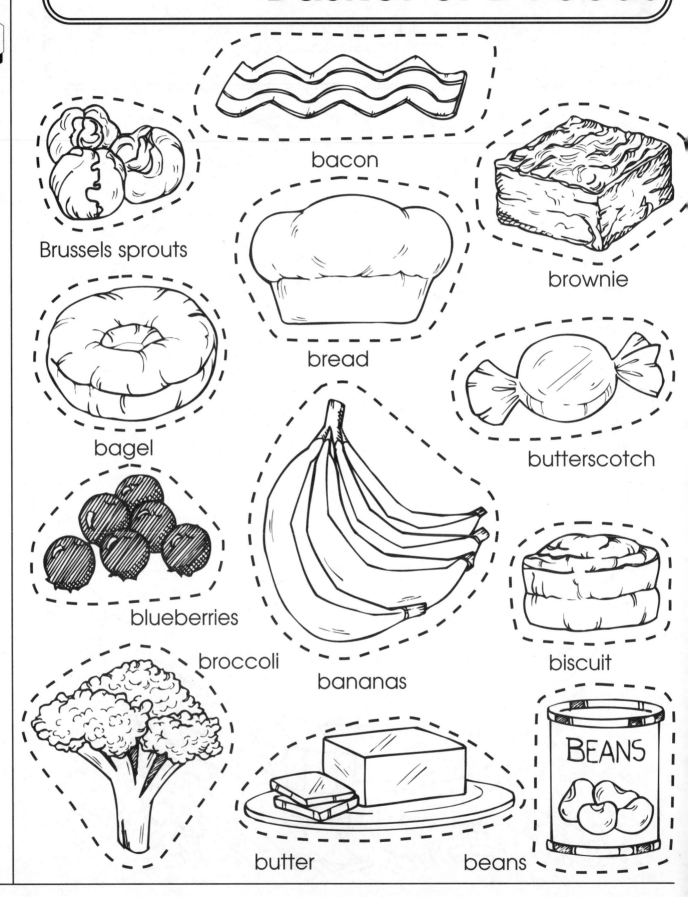

bacon

Brussels sprouts

brownie

bread

bagel

butterscotch

blueberries

bananas

biscuit

broccoli

butter

beans

# B Rummy

*Birds of a feather flock together,*
*And so will pigs and swine.*

**Getting Ready:** Mount rummy cards on light cardboard or heavy paper. If the cards are going to be used over and over, laminate or cover with clear adhesive paper. Cut along dotted lines.

**Directions:** This game can be played by two to four players. It is played like a simple version of Gin Rummy. Shuffle cards and deal each player seven cards. Place the other cards facedown in a stack. The top card is turned faceup. The first player can take the card turned faceup or draw from the top of the stack, then discards one card. The next player can take the top card or the card that has been discarded. Players take turns drawing and discarding until one player can make a set of four matching cards plus a set of three matching cards.

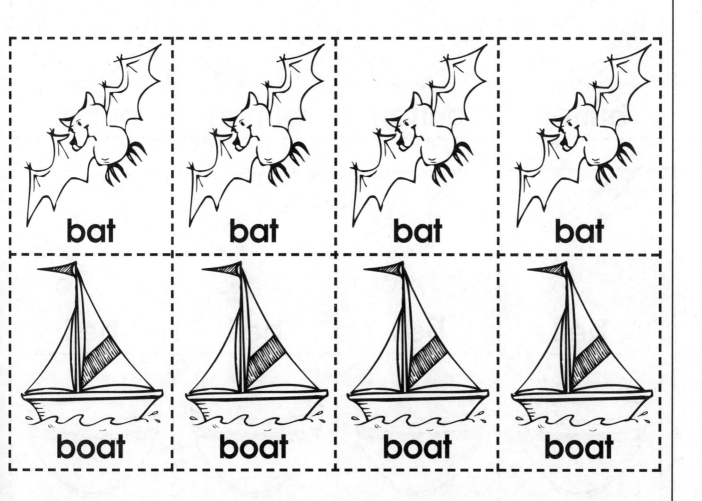

# B Rummy

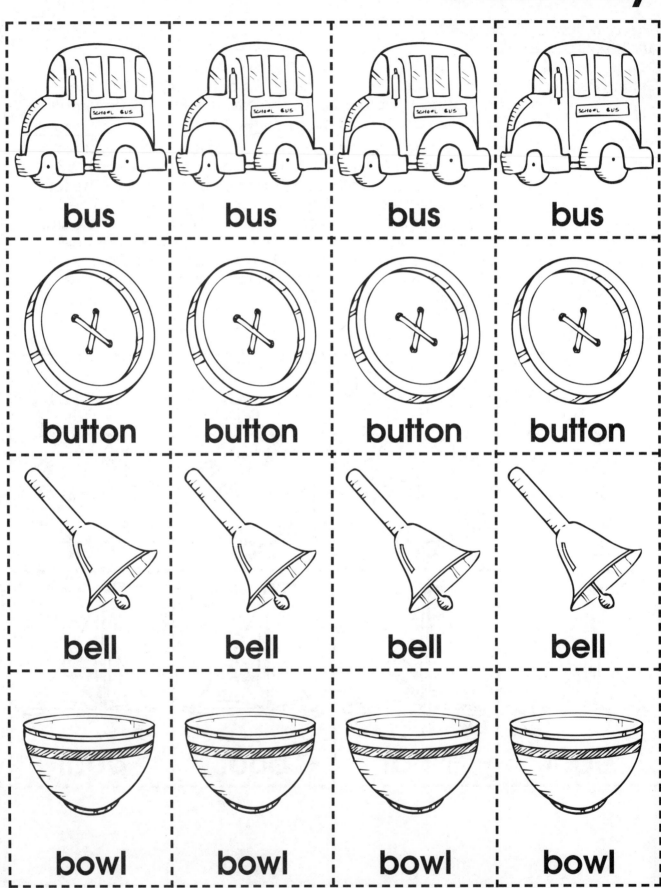

| | | | |
|---|---|---|---|
| bus | bus | bus | bus |
| button | button | button | button |
| bell | bell | bell | bell |
| bowl | bowl | bowl | bowl |

# B Rummy

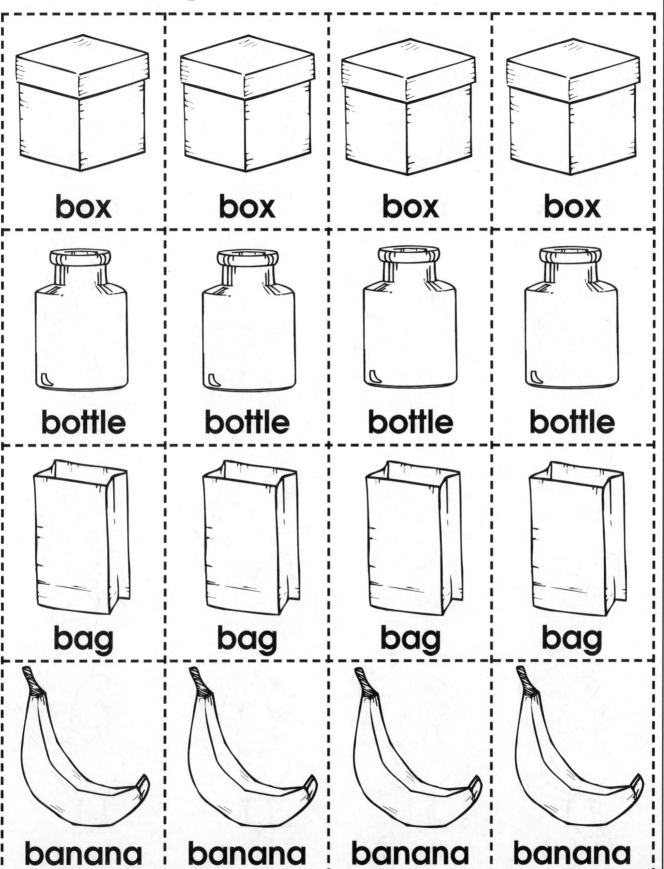

| box | box | box | box |
| bottle | bottle | bottle | bottle |
| bag | bag | bag | bag |
| banana | banana | banana | banana |

# B Rummy

**Game**

| | | | |
|---|---|---|---|
| book | book | book | book |
| bee | bee | bee | bee |
| bug | bug | bug | bug |
| bird | bird | bird | bird |

# B Rummy

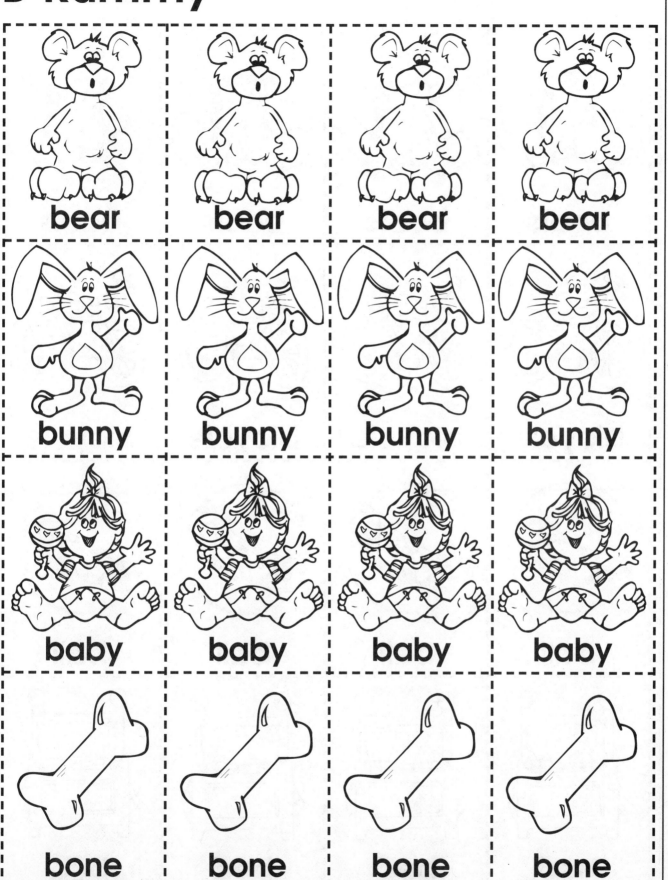

**bear** | **bear** | **bear** | **bear**

**bunny** | **bunny** | **bunny** | **bunny**

**baby** | **baby** | **baby** | **baby**

**bone** | **bone** | **bone** | **bone**

Game

TLC10000 Copyright © Teaching & Learning Company, Carthage, IL 62321

B

# B Rummy

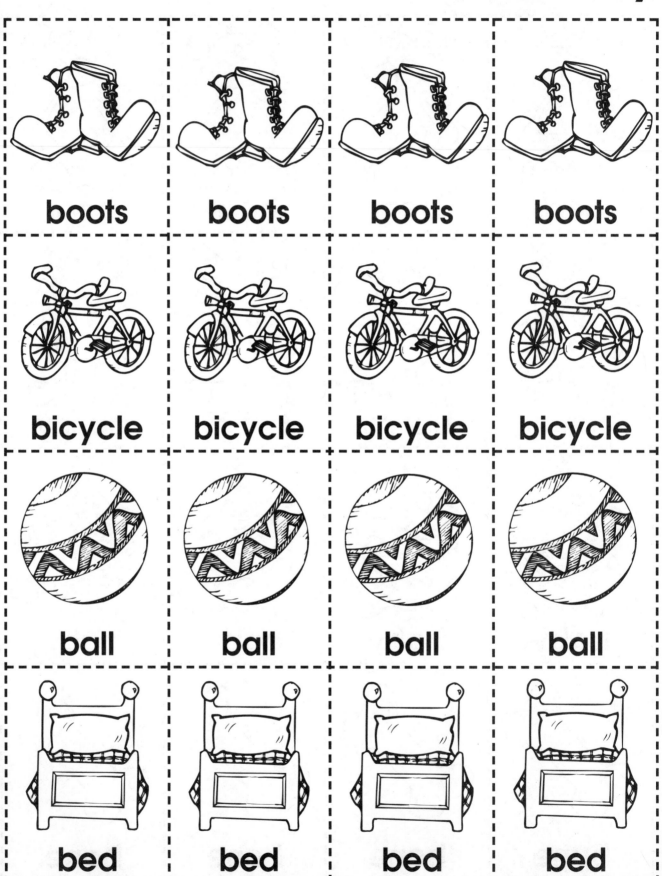

| boots | boots | boots | boots |
| bicycle | bicycle | bicycle | bicycle |
| ball | ball | ball | ball |
| bed | bed | bed | bed |

# Go Bananas!

**U**se bananas to make stuffed bananas or frozen bananas–easy and nutritious–and what a tasty way to celebrate the letter **B**!

## Banana Cream

Fiji

1. Have each student peel a banana and place in a bowl.
2. Mash bananas until smooth and completely without lumps.
3. Stir in 2 tablespoons (30 ml) coconut milk* and the juice of $1/8$ of a lemon or lime.  Stir until the mixture is thick.
4. Chill until serving.

\* Available in some specialty stores or departments.  If you cannot find it, use regular milk.

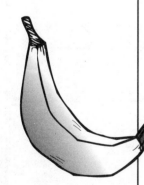

## Banana Loaf

Zimbabwe

1. Preheat oven to 350°F (177°C).  Grease a large loaf pan with butter.
2. Peel and mash 4 ripe bananas.  Add 1 teaspoon (5 ml) lemon juice.
3. Cream $1/2$ cup (120 ml) butter, $1/2$ cup (120 ml) brown sugar and 2 eggs.  Stir in 1 cup (240 ml) flour; 1 teaspoon (5 ml) baking powder and 2 tablespoons (30 ml) sour milk, yogurt or buttermilk.
4. Add this creamy mixture to the bananas.  Stir in $1/2$ cup (120 ml) chopped mixed nuts, if desired.
5. Pour mixture in prepared pan and bake for 1 hour, or until a knife inserts into the loaf comes out clean.  Remove from pan while warm.  Cool.  Slice.  Spread with butter.

**B**

# Beautiful Work!

_____

knows the shapes of the
uppercase and lowercase **B**.

*Blue Ribbon for You*
You know the sounds of the letter **B**.

**To:** _____

**Y**ou can read these words
that begin with **B**.

| | |
|---|---|
| ☐ bee | ☐ bug |
| ☐ button | ☐ bell |
| ☐ bowl | ☐ book |
| ☐ bottle | ☐ box |
| ☐ bat | ☐ boat |
| ☐ bus | ☐ bird |
| ☐ bag | ☐ banana |
| ☐ bear | ☐ bunny |
| ☐ buffalo | ☐ beaver |

# Top Banana!

To: _____

From: _____

# Cc

Charley Warley had a cow,
Black and white about the brow,
Open the gate and let her through,
Charley Warley's old cow!

Come, my dear children,
Up is the sun,
Birds are all singing,
And morn has begun.

Up from the bed, Miss,
Out on the lea;
The horses are waiting
For you and for me!

Cantaloupes!
Cantaloupes!
What is the price?
Eight for a dollar,
And all very nice.

# Come Up, Go Down

**Circle Time**

**U**se this rhyme as a springboard for discussing morning (and morning things, like the sun coming up) and evening (and evening things, like the sun going down).

This discussion can take a number of different directions. Here are a few examples.

### Morning/Evening Routines
Ask children to describe their morning and evening routines. Make a list–When do they get up? What do they do next? Make a graph–How many students are brushing their teeth at the same time? Talk about Nature's morning and evening routines (sun rising/setting, birds singing/resting, flowers opening/closing, what else?).

### Up/Down and Opposites
How many opposite pairs can your students name? Try acting them out. Label all the opposites in your classroom.

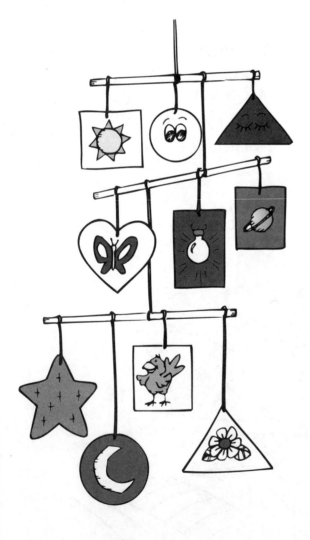

### Morning/Evening Mobile
Take one sheet of white paper and glue it to the same size sheet of black paper. Give each child a piece about 4" (10.16 cm) square. Children can cut their pieces into a shape if they desire. Children then draw (or cut out and paste) pictures of daytime things on the white side and night-time things on the black side. Punch a hole in the top of each child's finished work and tie on a string. Hang the pieces from a coat hanger or create a more elaborate suspension system (the cardboard tubing from some coat hangers works well). Vary the lengths of string to balance the mobile.

38

# Letter C Crayon Resist

**C**rayon resist is a technique of painting. Begin by having children use a white crayon to draw and color several letter **C**s on their papers. It is important to cover the letters with a thick layer of crayon. Prepare a thin mix of black tempera paint. Place the drawings on newspaper. Let children lightly brush one coat of paint over the whole picture. The letter **C**s will resist the paint and show up white. Let dry before removing from newspapers.

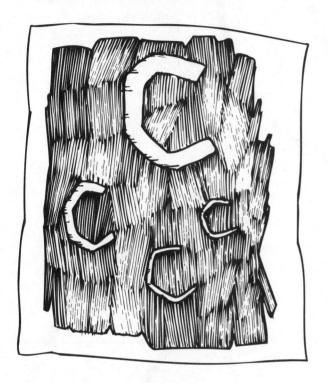

**A**fter children become familiar with this technique, they may want to make other crayon-resist pictures. Encourage them to make another crayon resist, this time of a **C** animal.

**Examples:**

| | |
|---|---|
| cow | chimpanzee |
| cat | camel |
| chipmunk | chicken |
| clam | cobra |
| cheetah | cougar |

**Pattern Activity**

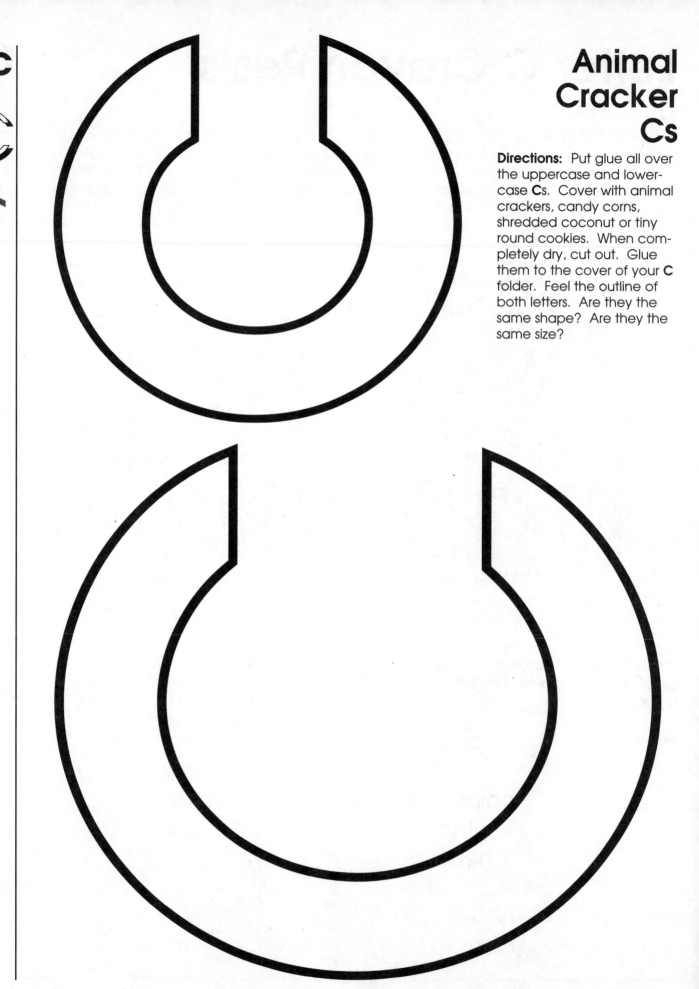

# Animal Cracker Cs

**Directions:** Put glue all over the uppercase and lowercase **C**s. Cover with animal crackers, candy corns, shredded coconut or tiny round cookies. When completely dry, cut out. Glue them to the cover of your **C** folder. Feel the outline of both letters. Are they the same shape? Are they the same size?

# Hiding Cs in the Icing

**U**se markers and crayons to put the icing and decorations on the desserts that begin with the letter **C** below: cake, cookies, candy, cupcake, caramels and custard. As you work, see how many letter **C**s you can hide in your designs.

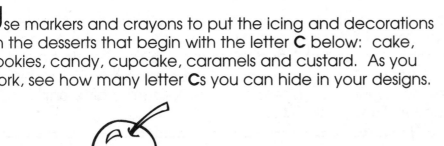

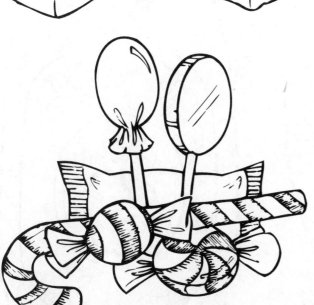

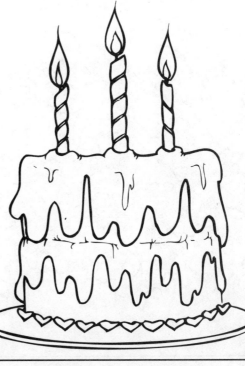

# Picnic of Cs

The letter **C** makes two sounds. It can sound hard like the letter **K** or soft like the letter **S**. Cut out and sort the foods below and on page 43 into two stacks: those that begin with the soft sound of **S** and those that begin with the hard sound of **K**. Color each food. Arrange one group of foods on a large paper plate and attach them with glue. Arrange the other foods on a different paper plate and attach them with glue, too.

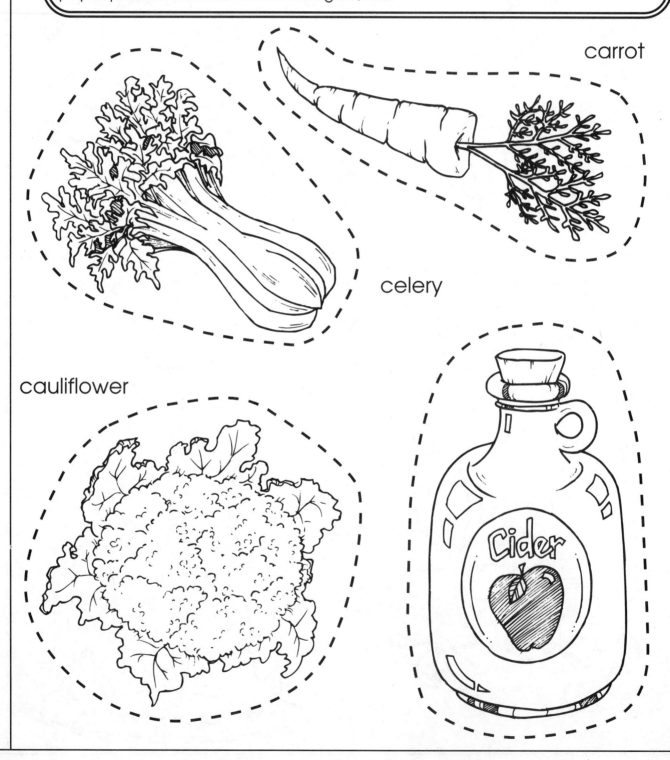

carrot

celery

cauliflower

Cider

# Picnic of Cs Patterns

cereal

corn

cucumber

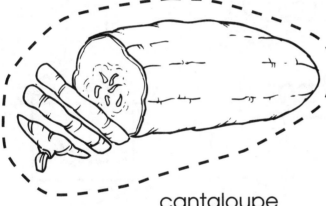

cantaloupe

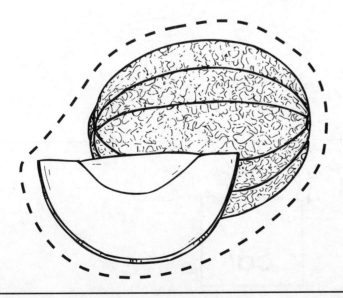

cabbage

Cc

Puzzle

# Cans of Cs

**A**ttach this page to construction paper or light cardboard. Cut out each picture word tab. (If you want to laminate the word cards and the cans on the next page, it's easier to do so *before* you cut out the items.) Use with the next page.

coffee

car

candle

cow

cat

c



TLC10000 Copyright © Teaching & Learning Company, Carthage, IL 62321

# Cans of Cs

Attach this page to construction paper or light cardboard. Cut out each can. Cut along the dotted lines at the top of each can. Have children insert the appropriate picture word tab in each can.

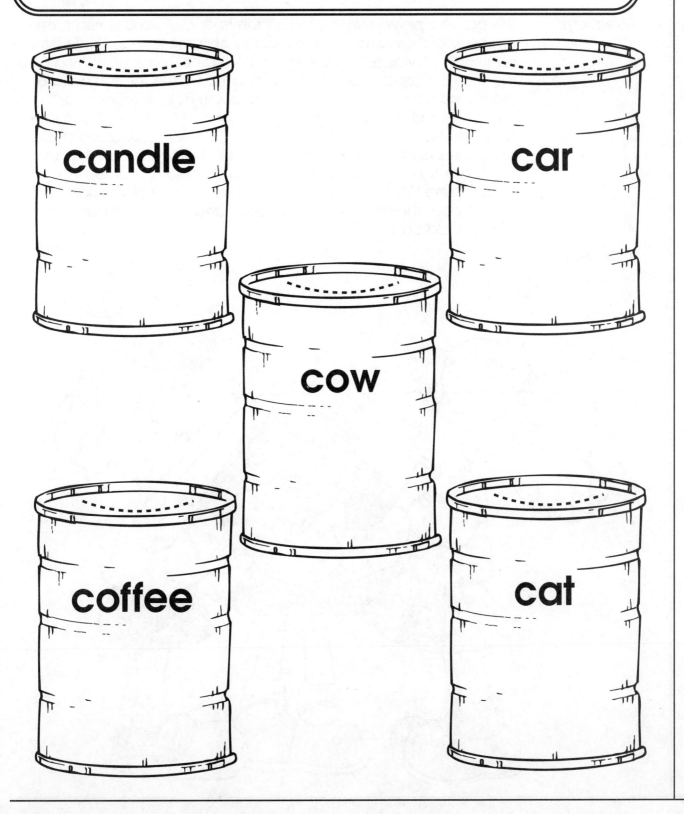

# Open the Gate, Charley

*Charley Warley had a cow,*
*Black and white about the brow,*
*Open the gate and let her through*
*Charley Warley's old cow!*

**Directions:** This game is played similar to London Bridge. Two children form a bridge with their arms. The rest of the children line up single file behind the "bridge." Children run under the "bridge" singing (Use the tune of "London Bridge.") the rhyme. When the last word of the rhyme is said, the bridge comes down trapping one child inside. That child must name an animal that begins with the letter **C**. When he does, the gate opens (children lift their arms) and the line moves again while everyone sings the new rhyme substituting the **C** animal named. Example: If the child says "camel," the verse is sung like this. Charley Warley had a camel, Black and white about the brow, Open the gate and let her through, Charley Warley's old camel!

**Examples:**

| | | |
|---|---|---|
| cow | clam | camel |
| cat | cheetah | chicken |
| chipmunk | chimpanzee | cobra |
| | | cougar |

# Cakes and Candy

*Charley loves good cake and ale,*
*Charley loves good candy.*

## Chocolate Peanut Raisin Clusters

### Mexico

Melt $1/2$ pound (.225 kg) sweet chocolate chips in a microwave. Stir in $1/2$ cup (120 ml) peanuts and $1/2$ cup (120 ml) seedless raisins. Drop mixture by spoonfuls onto waxed paper. Chill until firm.

## Apple Cheesecake

### Italy

1. Preheat oven to 400°F (204°C). Butter a round cake tin and sprinkle with flour.
2. Beat 2 egg yolks and $1/2$ cup (120 ml) sugar until thick. Mix the egg and sugar mixture with 1 cup (240 ml) Ricotta cheese, 1 tablespoon (15 ml) vanilla, 6 tablespoons (90 ml) orange juice and 1 teaspoon (5 ml) orange rind. Sift in 1 tablespoon (15 ml) baking powder. Stir in 1 cup (240 ml) apple pie filling. Pour batter into the prepared pan. Bake about 40 minutes. When the top of the cake is brown, turn off the heat, slightly open the oven door and leave the cheesecake to cool in the oven. (This will prevent the cake from sagging in the center.)
3. When cool, turn out to serve. Cake is best served cool but not cold. Sprinkle with confectioners' sugar or serve with whipped cream.

## Chocolate Cake

### Poland

1. Melt 1 cup (240 ml) milk chocolate in microwave.
2. Grind $2/3$ cup (160 ml) almonds. Mix 6 egg yolks with $2/3$ cup (160 ml) sugar and beat until the mixture is white. Add the melted chocolate to the sugar and egg mixture and beat until smooth. Add the almonds.
3. Beat the egg whites until stiff and gently fold into the mixture. Pour into two buttered loaf pans and bake in 275°F (135°C) oven for 55 minutes, or until a toothpick inserted in the center comes out clean. Remove from oven and cool slightly in the tins. Carefully remove from tins.
4. Use instant chocolate pudding, whipped cream or vanilla ice cream for filling between layers and icing on top. Sprinkle with grated chocolate.

*Certificate of Award*

_____

knows the shapes of the
uppercase and lowercase **C**.

# Congratulations!

You know the sounds the letter **C** makes.

**To:** _____

# Cool!

**Y**ou can read these
words that begin
with **C**.

☐ cake    ☐ cup
☐ car    ☐ cat
☐ corn    ☐ candy
☐ can    ☐ cow
☐ cantaloupe

*I'm certainly proud
of the careful
work you have
done
with the letter **C**.*

# Dd

**D**ickery, dickery, dock;
The mouse ran up the clock;
The clock struck One,
The mouse ran down,
Dickery, dickery, dock.

**D**ance, Thumbkin, dance;
Dance, ye merrymen, everyone;
For Thumbkin he can dance alone,
Thumbkin he can dance alone.

Dance, Foreman, dance;
Dance, ye merrymen, everyone;
But Foreman he can dance alone,
Foreman he can dance alone.

Dance, Longman, dance;
Dance, ye merrymen, everyone;
For Longman he can dance alone,
Longman he can dance alone.

Dance, Ringman, dance;
Dance, ye merrymen, dance;
But Ringman cannot dance alone,
Ringman he cannot dance alone.

Dance, Littleman, dance;
Dance, ye merrymen, dance;
But Littleman he can dance alone,
Littleman he can dance alone.

**D**eedle, deedle, dumpling, my son
   John,
Went to bed with his stockings on;
One shoe off, and one shoe on,
Deedle, deedle, dumpling, my son
   John.

# Dance, Thumbkin

**U**se indicated hand motions to turn the rhyme into a finger play.

| | |
|---|---|
| *Dance, Thumbkin, dance;* | (Tuck in fingers, wiggle thumb.) |
| *Dance, ye merrymen, everyone;* | (Wiggle all fingers and thumbs.) |
| *For Thumbkin he can dance alone,* | (Wiggle only the thumbs.) |
| *Thumbkin he can dance alone.* | (Wiggle only the thumbs.) |
| | |
| *Dance, Foreman, dance;* | (Wiggle only index fingers.) |
| *Dance, ye merrymen, everyone;* | (Wiggle all fingers and thumbs.) |
| *But Foreman he can dance alone,* | (Wiggle only index fingers.) |
| *Foreman he can dance alone.* | (Wiggle only index fingers.) |
| | |
| *Dance, Longman, dance;* | (Wiggle only middle fingers.) |
| *Dance, ye merrymen, everyone;* | (Wiggle all fingers and thumbs.) |
| *For Longman he can dance alone,* | (Wiggle only middle fingers.) |
| *Longman he can dance alone.* | (Wiggle only middle fingers.) |
| | |
| *Dance, Ringman, dance;* | (Wiggle only ring fingers.) |
| *Dance, ye merrymen, dance;* | (Wiggle all fingers and thumbs.) |
| *But Ringman cannot dance alone,* | (Wiggle only ring fingers.) |
| *Ringman he cannot dance alone.* | (Wiggle only ring fingers.) |
| | |
| *Dance, Littleman, dance;* | (Wiggle only little fingers.) |
| *Dance, ye merrymen, dance;* | (Wiggle all fingers and thumbs.) |
| *But Littleman he can dance alone,* | (Wiggle only little fingers.) |
| *Littleman he can dance alone.* | (Wiggle only little fingers.) |

**A**fter children are familiar with the song and actions, draw simple faces on each of their fingers with a fine-tip, washable marker. Perform the action song again using the finger puppets.

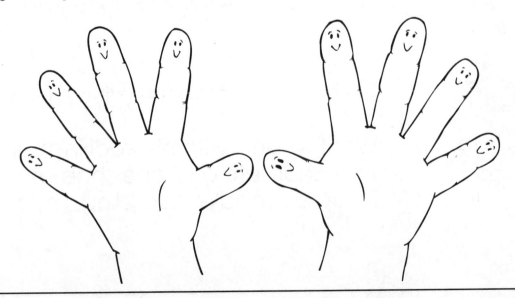

# Dickery, Dickery Clock

*Dickery, dickery, dock;*
*The mouse ran up the clock;*
*The clock struck One,*
*The mouse ran down,*
*Dickery, dickery, dock.*

**D**iscuss the sound the letter **D** makes as in *dickery* and *dock.* Recite the rhyme and then make a dickery clock. To make these clocks, have children color and cut out the clock face on the next page. Paste on a 7" (17.78 cm) paper plate. Color and cut out the mouse on the left. Paste to the center of clock. Cut out number stickers and paste in the appropriate spots on clock. Cut out clock hands and attach to the center of the clock with a brad fastener.

# Dickery, Dickery Clock

Craft

8  9  10  11  12

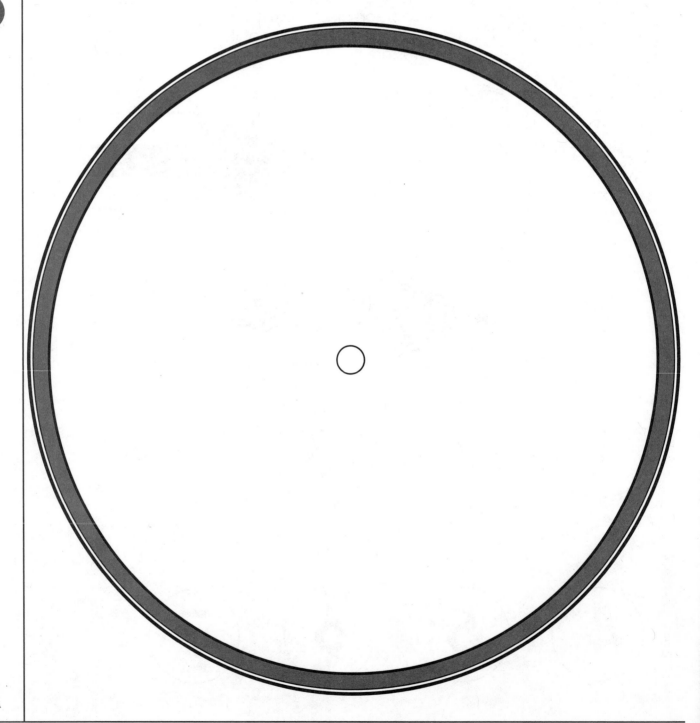

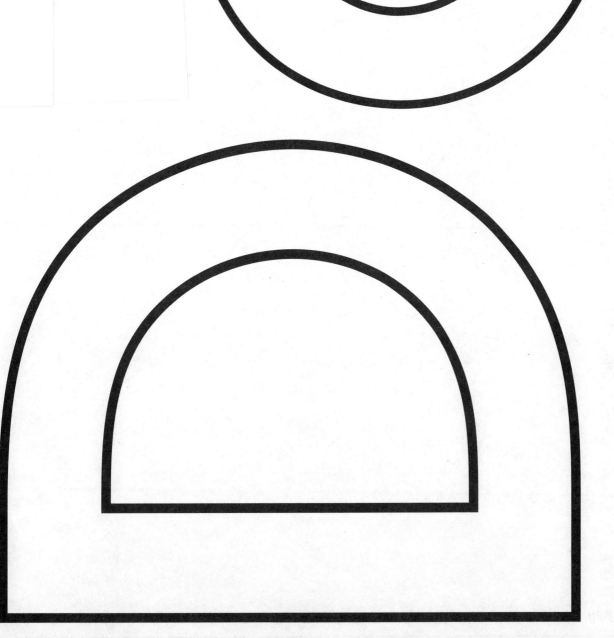

# D Is for Doodles

**W**hen people are bored, they often doodle. While talking on the telephone, many people scribble elaborate designs. Share your favorite doodle with the students. Then let them use the chalkboard to share their favorite doodles. Have each student tell about the doodle and discuss with the children when they doodle the most. Do they always doodle the same doodle? Do they doodle different doodles at certain times? Do their doodles tell about their feelings? After the discussion give each student a copy of the worksheet below. After drawing their favorite doodles, they can have friends doodle and autograph the sheet, too.

------------------------------------------------------------

D Is for Doodles•D Is for Doodles•D Is for Doodles•D Is for Doodles•D Is for Doodles

TLC10000 Copyright © Teaching & Learning Company, Carthage, IL 62321

# Dig Out the D Animals

You may see the mouse running up the clock, but can you find seven more animals hidden in the picture? Look closely and you will find these seven animals that begin with the letter **D**: dog, duck, deer, dinosaur, donkey, dolphin and dragon. Circle each animal and then color the picture.

D

# D Picture Dominoes

**Getting Ready:** Mount dominoes on light cardboard and then cut apart.

**Directions:** This game can be played by two to four players. Turn all the dominoes facedown and spread them out. Each player selects seven dominoes and places them faceup in front of him. The cards left facedown are called the bone pile. Turn over one domino from the bone pile. That is the beginning of the zoo train. The first player must play on either end of the train by placing a matching domino from his seven. A match is two of the same animal. Example: Players can put a deer on a deer, or a dog on a dog. If the player cannot make a match from the dominoes from his pile, he must keep drawing dominoes from the bone pile until he can make a match. Then the next player gets a turn. Players can add to either end of the domino zoo train. Players continue to build on the zoo train by making matches until one player has used all of her dominoes. If the bone pile is exhausted, players simply skip a turn if they cannot make a match.

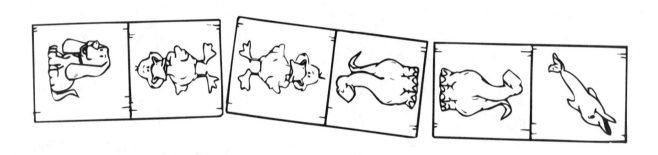

# D Picture Dominoes

# D Picture Dominoes

# D Picture Dominoes

# Delicious Dumplings

Dd

**Recipes**

*Deedle, deedle, dumpling, my son John,*
*Went to bed with his stockings on.*

## Salzburg Dumplings
### Austria

1. Preheat oven to 425°F (218°C). Butter a shallow baking dish. Beat 4 egg whites until stiff. Add 3 tablespoons (45 ml) sugar and 1 teaspoon (5 ml) vanilla to egg whites. Mix until the consistency of meringue.
2. Fold 3 egg yolks into the meringue. Sift $\frac{1}{8}$ cup (30 ml) flour over meringue and fold into the mixture. Spoon the mixture into buttered dish in three or four portions. Portions should be close together. Bake for 8-10 minutes. Serve immediately.

## Apple Dumplings
### Britain

In Britain they often serve apple dumplings. To make the following recipe you will need one apple for each student.

1. Let each student wash and peel her own apple. Plastic, serrated knives are sharp enough to cut and peel, yet safe enough for children to use. Teacher will have to core each apple. Don't cut the apples in pieces to remove core; leave apples whole.
2. To make the dumpling mix for each four apples, mix $\frac{2}{3}$ cup (160 ml) flour, a pinch of salt and $\frac{1}{3}$ cup (80 ml) butter until it resembles bread crumbs. Gradually add enough cold water to make a stiff dough. Divide into four pieces. On a floured board, roll out each piece of dough large enough to completely cover one apple.
3. Place apple on dough and fill the cavities with mixed dried fruit, lemon rind and brown sugar. Press the mixture down into the apple. Dampen the dough edges with water and press the joints firmly together. Place on a baking sheet with the joints on the underside. Repeat with each apple. Bake about 30 minutes in a 450°F (232°C) oven. Serve hot with vanilla ice cream or cold with whipped cream.

D

# DYNAMITE!

_____

knows the shapes of the
uppercase and lowercase **D**.

## _Delightful!_

You know the sounds the letter **D** makes.

**To:** _____

### Outstanding Domino Player!

To: _____

I'm delighted
with the
work you
have done
with the
letter _D_.

# Ee

**E**arly to bed and early to rise
Makes a man healthy, wealthy and wise.

**E**lsie Marley has grown so fine,
She won't get up to serve the swine;
But lies in bed till eight or nine,
And surely she does take her time.

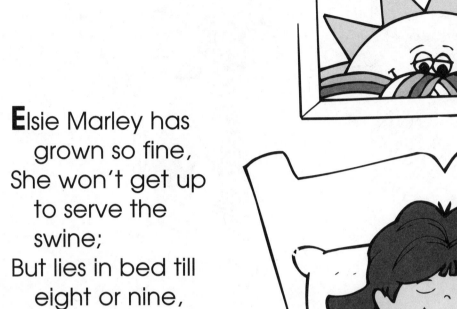

**E**ggs, butter, cheese, bread,
Stick, stock, stone, dead.

**Ee**

*Early to bed and early to rise
Makes a man healthy,
    wealthy and wise.*

**T**o practice learning all three **E** rhymes, play an echo game. Teacher says a word, phrase or line and the students echo it. The following rhyme is good to echo after every word:

Hello

*Eggs, butter, cheese, bread,
Stick, stock, stone, dead.*

(Repeat each word three times.)

**T**o learn the second rhyme, break it into phrases.

*Elsie Marley
    has grown so fine,
She won't get up
    to serve the swine;
But lies in bed
    till eight or nine,
And surely she does
    take her time.*

Elsie Marley, Marley, Marley
    has grown so fine, fine, fine,
She won't get up, up, up,
    to serve the swine, swine, swine;
But lies in bed, bed, bed
    till eight or nine, nine, nine,
And surely she does, does, does
    take her time, time, time.

**T**he third verse can be memorized by echoing the last word in each line.

*Early to bed and early to rise
Makes a man healthy, wealthy and wise.*

Rise, rise, rise
Wise, wise, wise.

E

# Ears and Eyes

**A**fter discussing ways we grow and how each body part gets bigger, have each student draw a self-portrait. Give each student a copy of an outline of an appropriately shaped face–round, oval, square. Provide small hand mirrors. Encourage each student to study his face in the mirror, paying special attention to his ears and eyes, and then draw and color his eyes and ears. Next add a nose, mouth and hair. If you choose, you can use the self-portraits to play a guessing game. Hold up portraits one at a time and let students guess who drew each one.

**E** is for my ears.
**E** is for my eyes.
**E** is for every part of me.
I'm perfect for my size.

**Discussion:** After completing the self-portraits, talk about the shapes of eyes and ears. What do we do with our eyes? Which grows the most after we are born, eyes or ears? Do we use our eyes at night while we are sleeping? Do we use our ears at night while we are dreaming?

## Pattern Activity

Ee

# E Creatures

**Directions:** Decorate the uppercase and lowercase Es with tiny bits of Styrofoam™ egg carton or crushed eggshells. Or glue large, movable craft eyes to each letter and add other features to make **E** creatures. Cut out the letters and glue them to the cover of your **E** folder. Run your fingers over the outlines. Which one has curved edges? Which one has straight edges? Which one has rounded openings? Which one has square openings? Which letter is the biggest?

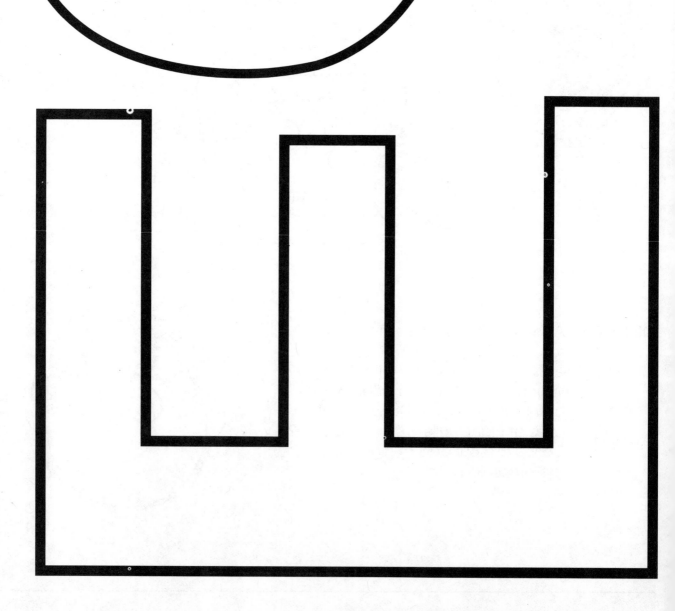

E

# E.L. Ephant

**H**ave students use the head and trunk patterns on the following page and the uppercase **E** below to make E.L. Ephant. Color and cut out patterns. Glue head and trunk where indicated. Fold the trunk on the dotted lines accordion-fashion. Use E.L. Ephant to celebrate **E** and have an autograph party. Let students collect signatures from people who have **E** in their names.

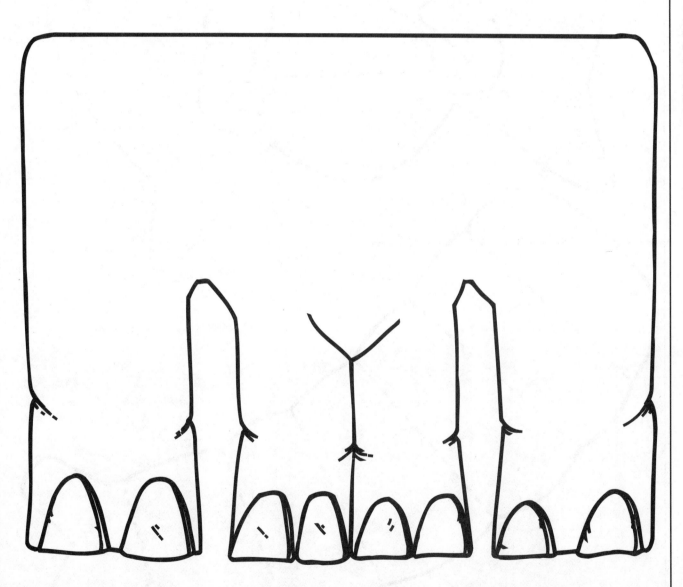

# E.L. Ephant Patterns

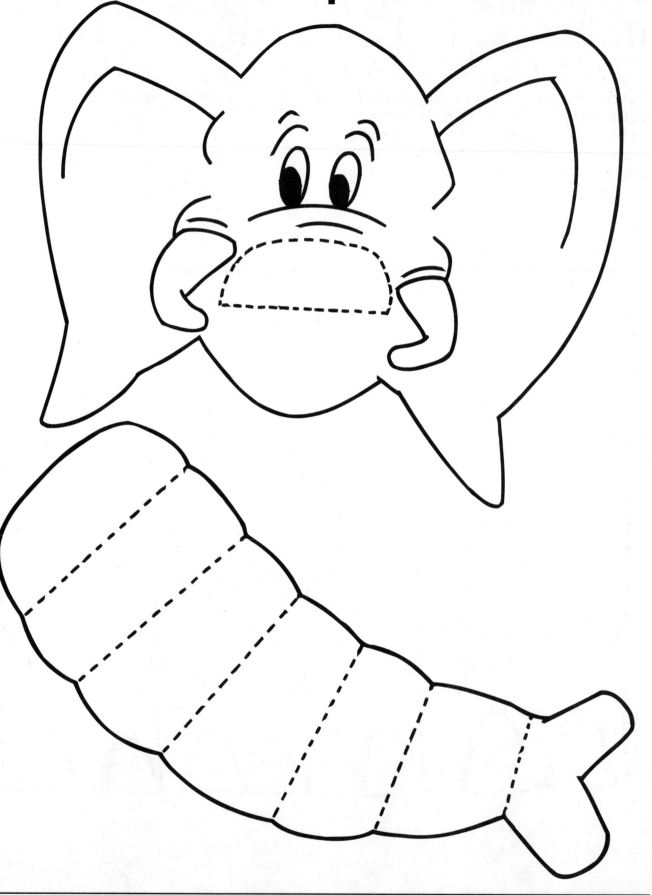

# The Eyes Have It

**C**ut and paste the eyes below on the **E** animals. Say the name of each animal. There is no right or wrong way to paste the eyes. Just have fun. Color the picture.

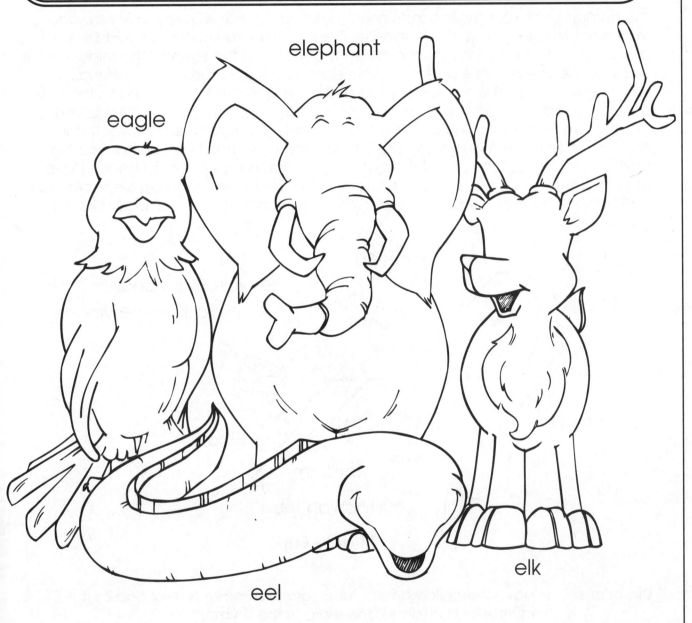

eagle

elephant

eel

elk

TLC10000 Copyright © Teaching & Learning Company, Carthage, IL 62321

# E Is for Ears

*Elsie Marley has grown so fine,*
*She won't get up to serve the swine;*
*But lies in bed till eight or nine,*
*And surely she does take her time.*

The human ear is an amazing instrument. Discuss the ear with the children. You may want to explain that the human ear has three parts: outer ear, middle ear and inner ear. The outer ear is like a cup that catches the sound. The middle ear is a tiny piece of skin that is stretched tight like a drum over the auditory canal. When sound enters the ear, the eardrum vibrates and sends the sound to the tiniest bones in the body called the hammer, anvil and stirrup. These three tiny bones make up the inner ear. This is where sound meets the nerves and travels to the brain where it is given meaning. Discuss why some animals have better hearing than humans. Does the size of the outer ear make sounds easier to hear? Have the children cup their ears and see if they can hear better. Can an elephant hear better than a human? After discussing the importance of the ear, play a listening game.

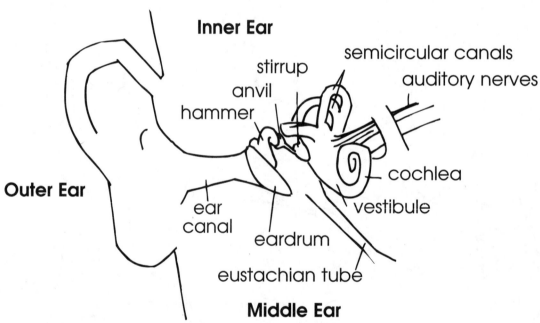

**Inner Ear**

semicircular canals

auditory nerves

stirrup

anvil

hammer

cochlea

**Outer Ear**

vestibule

ear canal

eardrum

eustachian tube

**Middle Ear**

**Directions:**  Have the children take turns saying a line or two of one of the **E** rhymes and change one word in the rhyme.

**Example:**  Early to bed and early to rise, Makes a *boy* healthy, wealthy and wise. Chilren take turns guessing which word was changed in the rhyme.

*Early to bed and early to rise*
*Makes a man healthy, wealthy and*
  *wise.*

*Eggs, butter, cheese, bread,*
*Stick, stock, stone, dead.*

# "Eggs"traordinary Recipes

*Eggs, butter, cheese, bread,*
*Stick, stock, stone, dead.*

## Baked Eggs
### Russia

1. Preheat oven to 375°F (191°C).
2. Place enough paper baking cups in cupcake baking tins for each student. Put 1 teaspoon (5 ml) of butter in the bottom of each baking cup. Grate cheddar cheese and sprinkle in the bottom of each paper cup. Add chopped ham. Drop 1 egg into each dish.
3. Bake in oven until set, about 15 minutes, or until firm, about 20 minutes.

## Deviled Eggs
### England

1. Peel hard-boiled eggs. Cut each one in half and carefully remove yolk.
2. In a small bowl, mash egg yolks with a fork. Add 1 tablespoon (15 ml) of mayonnaise for each egg used. Stir until creamy.
3. Spoon mixture back into egg white halves. Sprinkle with paprika.
4. Chill. Serve with bread or crackers.

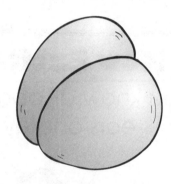

## Quiche Lorraine
### France

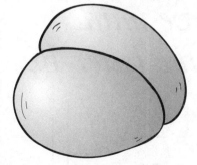

1. Place a ready-made pastry crust in a glass pie dish and bake for 5 minutes at 450°F (232°C). Remove from oven and let cool.
2. Beat 2 eggs and 1 cup (240 ml) cream. Pour mixture into prepared crust. Sprinkle with bacon bits or crumbled bacon. Bake in 375°F (191°C) oven for 30 minutes or until the top is rich brown.
3. Can be served hot, warm or cold.

# Extraordinary

_____

knows the shapes of the uppercase and lowercase **E**.

## Excellent

You know the long and short sounds the letter **E** makes.

**To:** _____

## How Exciting!

You know all about your ears and eyes.

_I'm very proud of the excellent effort you have made with the letter E._

# Ff

**F**ee, Fi, Fo, Fum!
I smell the blood of an Englishman:
Be he alive, or be he dead,
I'll grind his bones to make me bread.

**F** was a fox,
So cunning and sly:
Who looks at the hen-roost–
I need not say why.

Hen House

**L**ittle Tommy Grace had a pain in
   his face,
So bad he could not learn a letter;
When in came Dicky Long,
Singing such a funny song,
That Tommy laughed,
And found his face much better.

# Sing a Song of Foxes

*F was a fox,*
*So cunning and sly.*

**U**se the tune of "Ten Little Indians" to create new songs for celebrating **F**.

**Example:**
One little,
Two little,
Three little foxes.
Four little,
Five little,
Six little foxes.
Seven little,
Eight little,
Nine little foxes.
Ten little foxes here.

**Alternative:** To teach or reinforce counting to ten, this rhyme can be turned into an action song. Children are to hold up both hands with fingers down, forming two fists. Appropriate number of fingers are shown while singing each line of the song. Then take turns making up new songs by replacing foxes with other objects, especially animals, that begin with the letter **F**. Examples: fawn, fish, flea, firefly, fly, frog. After children have invented new verses for the song, instead of counting the animals that begin with **F**, make up verses that tell how they move. Youngsters make the appropriate movements as they sing the new songs, too.

**Example:**

Hop little,
Hop little,
Hop little frogs
Hop little,
Hop little,
Hop little frogs,
Hop to your lily pad.

Or,
Glow little firefly.
Leap little flea.
Swim little fish.
Run little fawn.
Fly little fly.

# Fingerprint F Things

**Craft**

**D**iscuss fingerprints.  Explain that everyone has different fingerprints.  Fingerprints are so unique that they are often used to identify people.  Have children use a stamp pad and large sheet of white construction paper to make their own finger-prints.  Provide soapy water and towels for cleanup.  Use magnifying glasses to examine the fingerprints more closely.  Then by adding details with fine-tip, wash-able markers, have students turn each fingerprint into an object that begins with the letter **F**.  Give the list of **F** things that follows to help students get started.

**Examples:**

fox
fan
feather
fern
flag
flake
fruit
fly
fawn
fish
flea
firefly
frog
fig
face
feet
fire
foot
flower

# Fruit Fun

**C**hildren can make beautiful gift wrapping paper, book covers, report folders and bulletin board trim with these easy-to-do fruit prints.

**Materials:**

fruit sliced in half (experiment with cutting horizontally and vertically)
tempera paint
paper plates or pie tins
white paper (large sheets for gift wrap, calculator tape for bulletin board borders)

**P**our paints into pie tins or paper plates.  Cut fruit in half.  Dip the cut side of the fruit into the paint.  Press carefully onto the paper.  Lift fruit and admire your print.

**A**pples and pears work the best.  Citrus fruit (oranges, lemons, limes) may need to have some of the juice squeezed out before they will hold the paint well.  Pulpy fruit (plums, mangoes, bananas) make interesting designs and textures but do not retain much of their identity.

**Variations:**  Dark paint colors on butcher paper make interesting patterns.  Bright colors (even neon) look great on newsprint.  Print a fruit salad on (uncoated) white paper plates and have a tea party!

# Fancy Fs

**Directions:** Use feathers, fur or fuzz to make the uppercase and lowercase **F**s fancy. Or decorate them with drawings of fireflies, fleas, frogs or fish. Cut out the letters and glue them on the cover of your **F** folder. How do they feel? Are they fluffy?

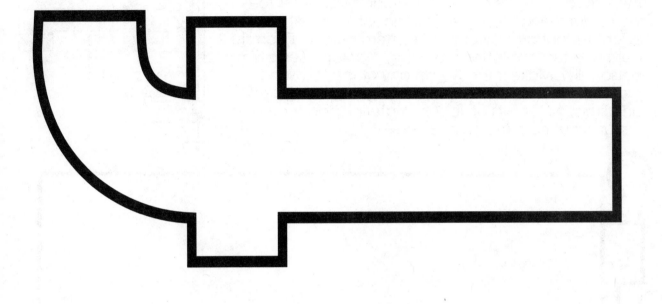

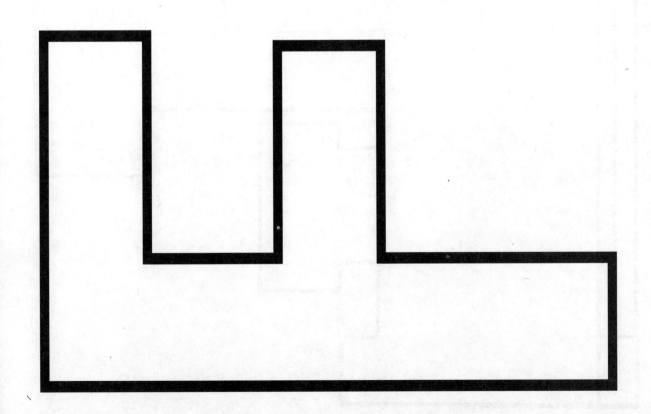

TLC10000 Copyright © Teaching & Learning Company, Carthage, IL 62321

# Fancy Me F Flags

*Fee, Fi, Fo, Fum!*
*I smell the blood of an Englishmen.*

**D**iscuss how flags are symbols for different countries or organizations. Look at the American flag and pictures of flags from other countries. Explain the meaning of the stars and stripes on the American flag. After talking about being English, American, Chinese, etc., give each student a copy of the **F** pattern below. Each student is to turn the letter into a flag that represents him personally. Make it fancy with any of the following: crayons, washable markers, paints, gummed stickers and stars, glitter, bits of ribbon, material, paper cutouts, pictures cut from magazines, etc.

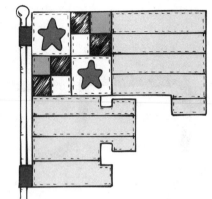

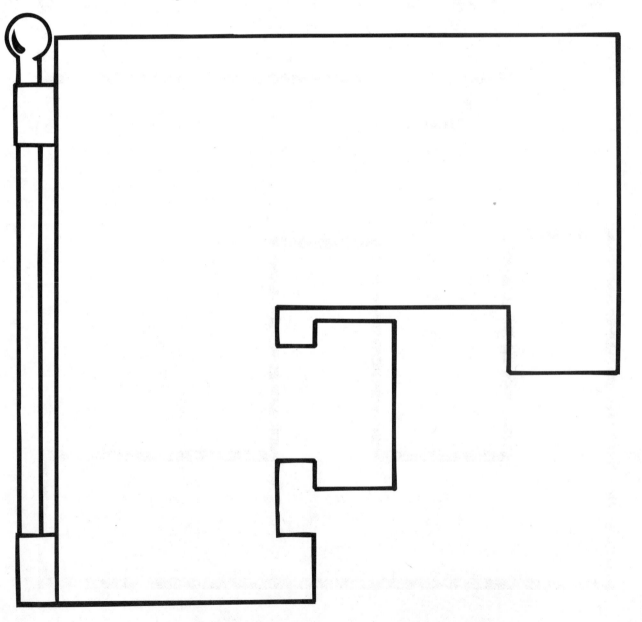

# Friends in the Fern Forest

**H**ow many things that begin with the letter **F**, besides the fox, can you find hidden in the forest? If you look closely, you will see a fawn, fish, firefly, fly, frog, fan, flag and face. Circle the **F** things and color the picture.

# Forest Friends

Color, cut out and paste the forest friends in an appropriate place in the picture. Two animals belong in the water, two belong on land and two belong in the air. When you are done pasting, color the rest of the picture.

# Funny Faces

*Little Tommy Grace had a pain in his face,*
*So bad he could not learn a letter;*
*When in came Dicky Long,*
*Singing such a funny song,*
*That Tommy laughed,*
*And found his face much better.*

**Getting Ready:** Your children will have fun playing this funny faces game. Here is what you'll need:

      spinner (cut out and attach arrow loosely with a brad fastener)
      a white paper plate for each player
      a collection of eyes, eyebrows, noses, mouths and ears (either cut from magazines or drawn by the children–see next page) placed in piles and organized by type (Page 196 has additional facial features you may want to use.)

**Directions:** Children determine who will go first. Players spin to see which face part they will choose. They make a selection and place it on the appropriate place on their paper plate "face." If a player spins but has already selected that face part, the play passes to the next player. The first person to complete a "funny face" is the winner.

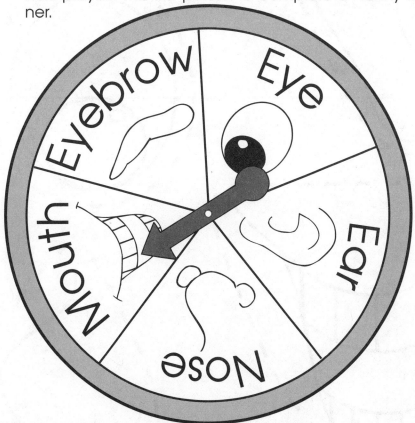

**Alternative:** This game works best with people features, but if your students are ready for a challenge, try animal faces.

# Funny Faces Patterns

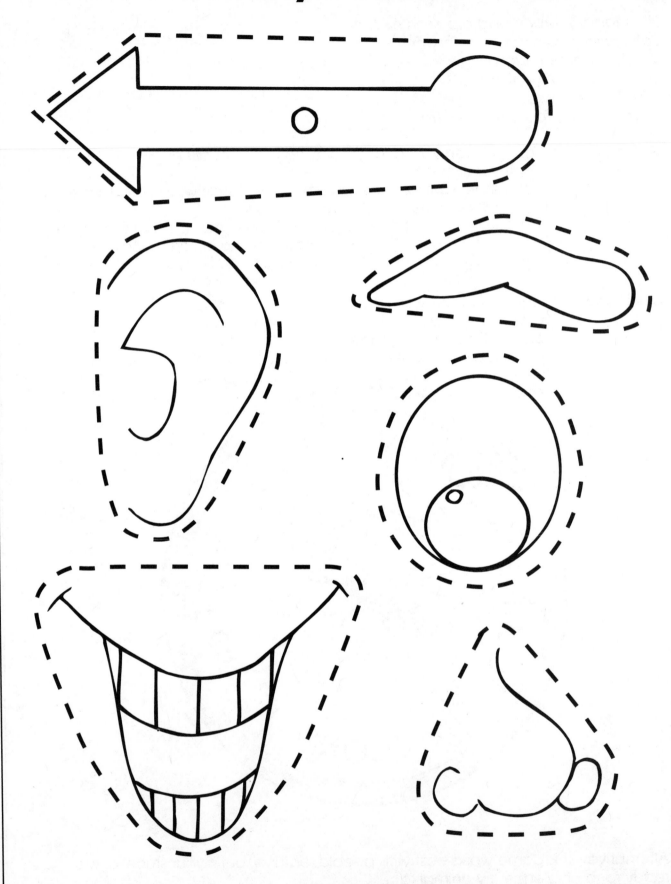

# Fancy, Fruity Foods

The fanciest food available comes already packaged when it is picked from trees, vines or bushes. Fruit! It's a healthy alternative to sugar-coated desserts. Celebrate fruit with your students with these flavorful recipes.

### Fruit Ices

Hawaii

1. In a blender, place 2 cups (480 ml) slightly thawed berries, 1 cup (240 ml) milk and 2 tablespoons (30 ml) sugar.
2. Blend until berries are smooth and creamy. Serve immediately. Makes 4 large drinks or 6 small ones.

### Favorite Fruit Salad

The Middle East

People living in the countries known as the Middle East, produce an enormously varied and healthy range of fresh vegetables and all kinds of fruits. Dried or fresh fruit is served as dessert. Make a big fruit salad full of everyone's favorites! Ask each student to bring one serving of his favorite fruit—an apple, a large slice of watermelon, half of a cantaloupe, a basket of berries, etc. Line up the fruits. First put them in a line according to size. Then place them in a line in alphabetical order. Group them according to color. Make sets of fruits that grow on trees, bushes, vines, etc. How else can the fruit be grouped? After the discussion, have each child prepare his piece of fruit for the salad. Peel, core, remove seeds and cut into bite-sized chunks. Mix together and serve.

# *Fine!*

_____

knows the shapes of the
uppercase and lowercase **F**.

# FANTASTIC!

You know the sounds the letter **F** makes.

**To:** _____

## Fabulous!

**Y**ou made a very
fancy **F** flag.

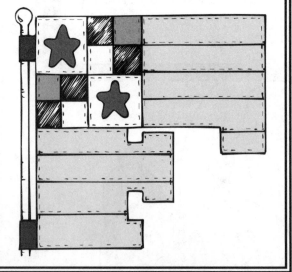

**I'm very fond of all
the fine work you
have finished with
the letter *F*.**

TLC10000 Copyright © Teaching & Learning Company, Carthage, IL 62321

# Gg

**G**ood people all, of every sort,
Give ear unto my song:
And if you find it wondrous short,
It cannot hold you long.

**G**reat A, little A,
This is pancake day;
Toss the ball high,
Throw the ball low,
Those that come after
May sing Heigh-ho!

**G**eorgey Porgey, pudding and pie,
Kissed the girls and made them cry;
When the girls came out to play,
Georgey Porgey ran away.

**G**oosey, goosey, gander,
Wither dost thou wander?
Upstairs, and downstairs, and
In my lady's chamber.

**G**ood horses, bad horses,
What is the time of day?
Three o'clock, four o'clock.
Now fare you away.

# Good People Give Ear

*Good people all, of every sort,*
*Give ear unto my song:*
*And if you find it wondrous short,*
*It cannot hold you long.*

The human body is the most extraordinary muscial instrument of all! It can make an infinite number of sounds. Explore some of these sounds with your class. Challenge the children to see how many different sounds they can make with their bodies. Examples: click tongue, drum face, slap hips, stomp feet, whistle, hum, clap and snap fingers. List the sounds on the board. Practice the different sounds so that the children can try them all! Assign a sound to each child or small group. As one child or small group recites a **G** rhyme, the others keep time with sounds they make with their bodies. As you lead the human orchestra, raise your hand for the sound to be louder, lower your hand to quiet the sounds. Children watch you for signals. How harmonic can the class become? Try all of these.

*Good horses, bad horses,*
*What is the time of day?*
*Three o'clock, four o'clock.*
*Now fare you away.*

*Goosey, goosey, gander,*
*Wither dost thou wander?*
*Upstairs, and downstairs, and*
*In my lady's chamber.*

*Georgey Porgey, pudding and pie,*
*Kissed the girls and made them cry;*
*When the girls came out to play,*
*Georgey Porgey ran away.*

# Goose, Goat and Gorilla

*Goosey, goosey, gander,*
*Wither dost thou wander?*
*Upstairs, and downstairs, and*
*In my lady's chamber.*

**D**iscuss the sound of the letter **G** as in *goosey*.
Recite the rhyme. Then make a stuffed felt goose or
another **G** animal. Each child will need a pattern
(see pages 88-90), felt, cotton balls or tissues for stuffing, needle and thread, yarn scraps, pencil, washable markers and scissors. Let each student choose
a color of felt she likes. She will need two pieces.

1. Place the pattern on top of the felt and use a
   pencil to trace around the outline.

2. Repeat this step again because each animal
   needs two sides.

3. Use a black marker to draw an eye on both
   pieces. Cut out on the outline.

4. Allow each student to sew around the edges
   as shown in the beginning and ending where it
   is indicated on the pattern. Stuff the opening
   of the animal with cotton balls or stuffing.

5. If student is making a goat, sew on loops of
   yarn for a tail. Put a loop of yarn on each animal for hanging.

6. Have an adult or older student sew around
   the rest of the animal to close.

# Gg

## Craft

# Goose Pattern

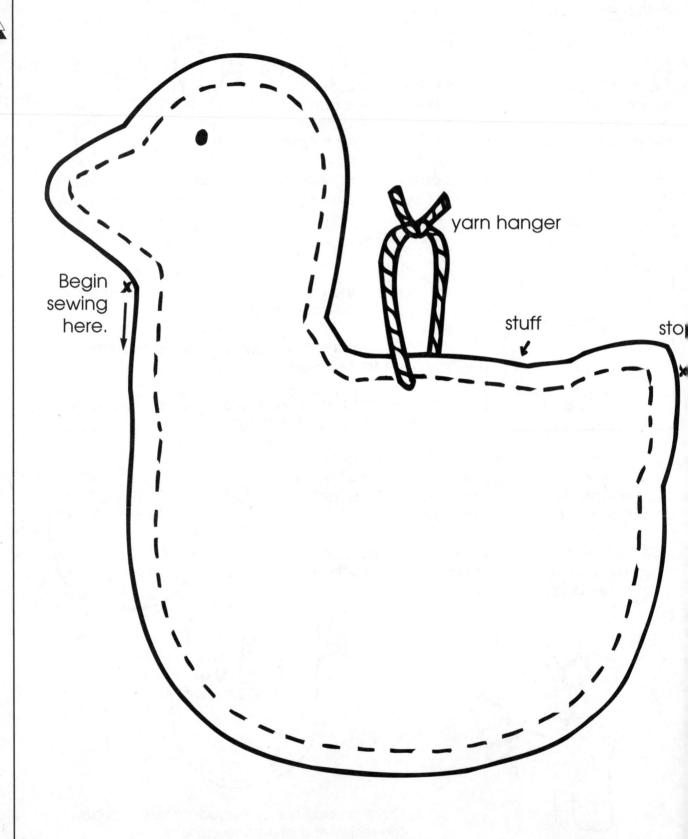

Begin sewing here.

yarn hanger

stuff

sto[p]

# Goat Pattern

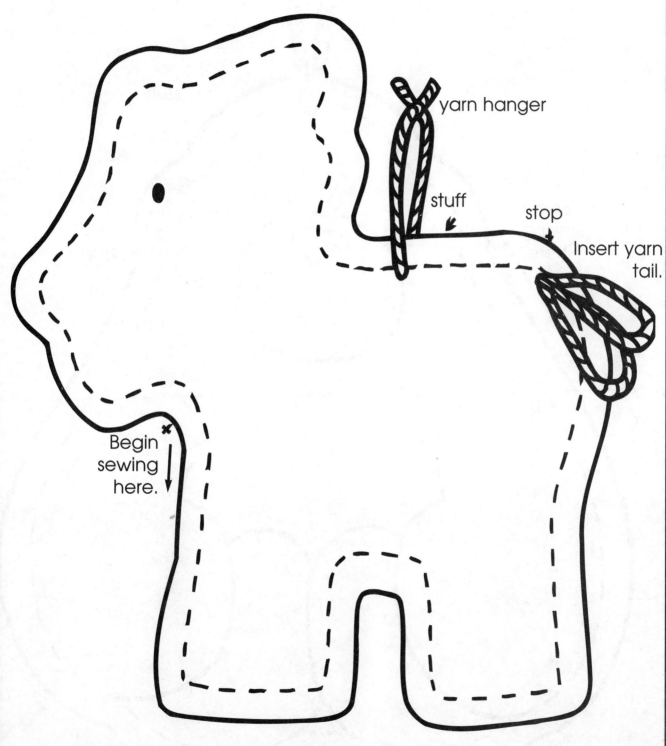

yarn hanger

stuff

stop

Insert yarn tail.

Begin sewing here.

# Gorilla Pattern

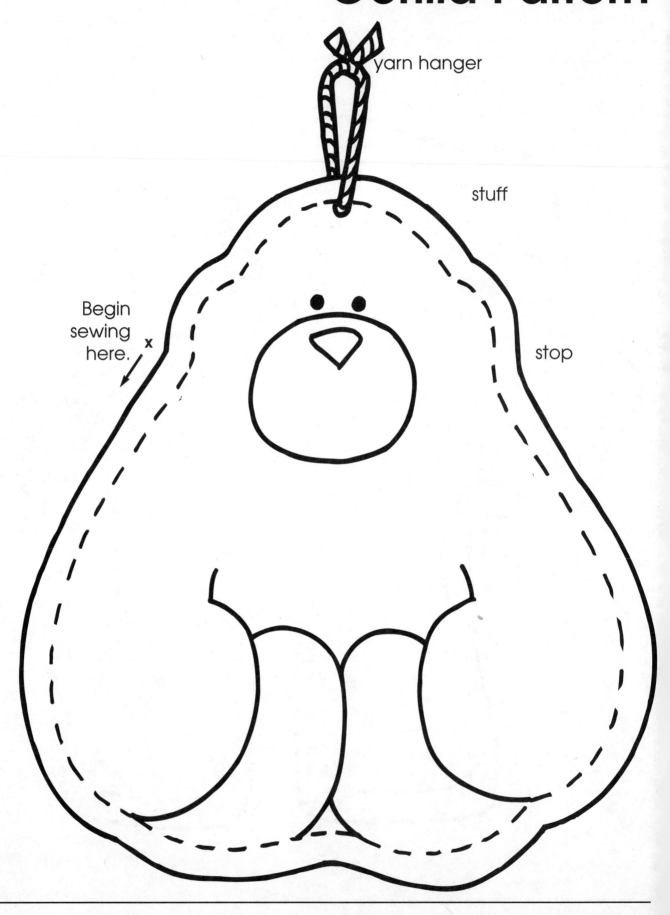

yarn hanger

stuff

Begin
sewing
here. **x**

stop

# Glittery Gs

**Directions:** Use green, gold and gray (silver) glitter to decorate the **G**s. You can make them striped, solid, spotted or any design you choose. Plan your pattern before you begin putting on glue and glitter. When dry, cut out letters and attach them to your **G** folder. Touch each letter. How do they feel?

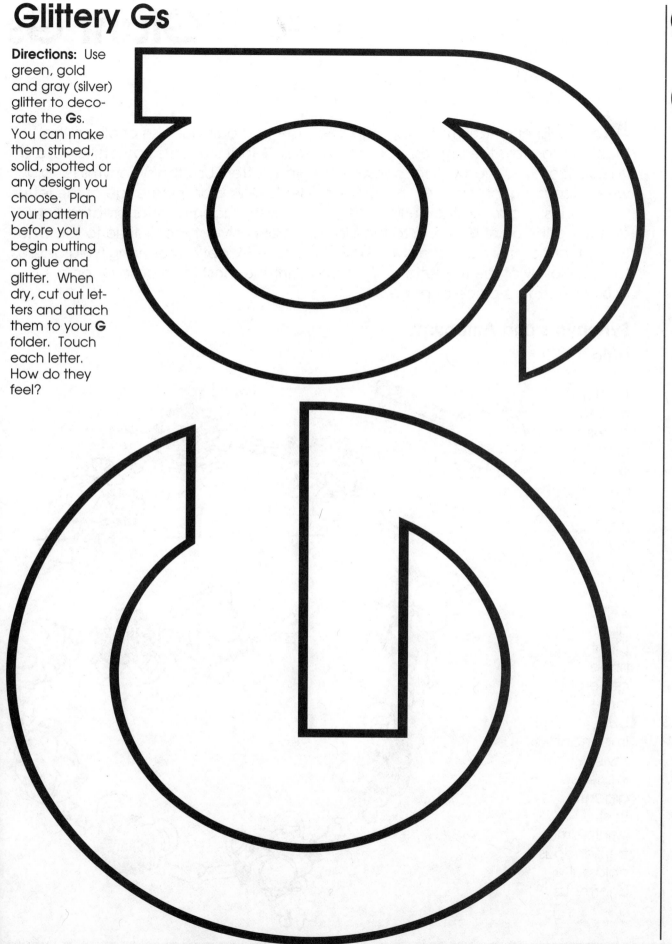

**Pattern Activity**

## Writing Idea

*Great A, little A,*
*This is pancake day.*

**M**ake a list of synonyms for *big* and *little*. Then go outside. Use chalk on the blacktop to draw the biggest uppercase letter **G** that students can make. Use a yardstick or tape measure to measure the giant letter. Use the synonyms for *big* when discussing the giant **G**. Have the students walk along the edge of the letter. Hold hands and make the outline of the letter with students. After creating and discussing the giant **G**, return to the classroom and give students time to see who can write the littlest lowercase **G**. How tiny can they get? Use mangifying glasses to look closely at the tiny letters. Who can print the most lowercase **G**s on a 1" (2.54 cm) square piece of paper?

### Synonyms and Antonyms

#### Little
tiny
small
minute
minuscule
lean
slight
narrow
wee
petite
trivial

#### Big
great
giant
huge
generous
large
bulky
important
lavish
immense
gigantic
vast
infinitesimal
tremendous
colossal
enormous

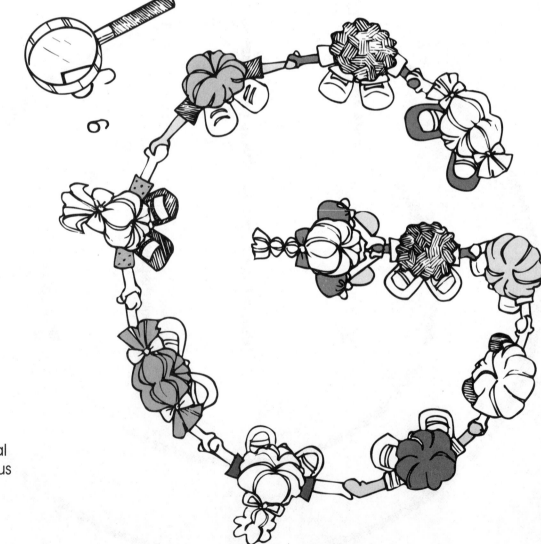

# Green, Gold or Gray?

Use the color code to color each space.

green •      gold ••      gray •••

# Good Horses, Bad Horses

*Good horses, bad horses,*
*What is the time of day?*
*Three o'clock, four o'clock.*
*Now fare you away.*

**Directions:**  Good Horses, Bad Horses is an out-of-doors running, tag game. Divide the class in half. One half of the children are "horses," the other half are "trees." Place the "trees" about 6' (1.82 m) from each other so that there is space to run between them. As the "trees" stand grounded in a spot, the "horses" chant the rhyme and run in and around them. The "trees" reach out with their branches (arms) and try to tag "horses" that run by. If a "horse" is tagged, he becomes a "tree" and must stay in place. After a while the teacher blows a whistle and everyone freezes. When she blows the whistle a second time, the "trees" become "horses," and the "horses" become "trees." Game continues as the "horses" chant and run through the new "trees." Play until the children tire of the game.

**Variation:**  The rhyme can also be used to begin a race. The two runners chant the rhyme and when they get to the last word, *away*, the race is on!

**Directions:**  Use the rhyme "Georgey Porgey" to play a tag game, too. Choose three children to be Georgey Porgeys and one student to be the fairy. As children run around, the Georgey Porgeys try to tag students. If a student is tagged, he is grounded and makes a crying sound to let the fairy know that he has been caught. When the fairy taps a child with the magic wand (drinking straw) he is free again.

# Ginger Goodies

G is for ginger. Spice up snacks with any of the three ginger recipes that follow. Serve with ginger ale, of course!

### Gingerbread Pictures

Give each child a graham cracker. Provide vanilla icing and a variety of decorations. Spread icing on each graham cracker and decorate with raisins, bits of dried fruit, chocolate chips or small candies and create a gingerbread picture.

### Gingerbread and Cream

Germany

To make a quick gingerbread, use a boxed gingerbread mix. Follow the directions on the package. Can be baked in an oven, microwave or even cooked on a stove top if you have a tight-fitting lid. Serve warm with whipped cream or sprinkle with confectioners' sugar.

### Gingersnap Sandwiches

Jamaica

Ginger is grown in Jamaica and often used to season many Jamaican dishes. Celebrate the flavor of ginger by spreading vanilla icing or peanut butter on two gingersnap cookies and put together sandwich-fashion. Or create a tasty dessert sandwich by placing sliced apples, pears, bananas or peaches between two gingersnaps.

# GREAT!

_____

knows the shapes of the uppercase and lowercase **G**.

_Good!_

You know the sounds the letter **G** makes.

**To:** _____

## Outstanding!

**Y**ou made a great **G** animal.

## I'm glowing over the work you have done with the letter G.

# Hh

**H**ush-a-bye, baby, on the treetop,
When the wind blows, the cradle will
   rock;
When the bough bends, the cradle
   will fall.
Down will come baby, cradle and
   all.

**H**ub a dub, dub,
Three men in a tub;
The butcher, the baker,
The candlestick maker.

**H**eigh, diddle, diddle,
   The cat and the fiddle,
      The cow jumped over the
         moon;
      The little dog laughed
      To see such sport,
         And the dish ran away
            with the spoon.

**H**umpty Dumpty sat on a wall.
Humpty Dumpty had a great fall.
All the King's horses and all the
   King's men
Couldn't put Humpty Dumpty
   together again.

# Hand Jive

**E**xplain to the students that in hand jive you use your hands to make the motions that tell the words of the song or rhyme. Use hand jives to perform the rhyme.

*Hush-a-bye, baby, on the treetop,*     (Rock an imaginary baby.)
*When the wind blows, the cradle will rock;*     (Puff out cheeks and blow, rock cradle.)
*When the bough bends, the cradle will fall.*     (Hold arms overhead, drop arms to side.)
*Down will come baby, cradle and all.*     (Pretend to catch baby and rock.)

**T**ry some body jive for one of the other **H** rhymes.

*Heigh, diddle, diddle,*
*The cat and the fiddle,*
*The cow jumped over the moon;*
*The little dog laughed*
*To see such sport,*
*And the dish ran away with the spoon.*

*Humpty Dumpty sat on a wall.*
*Humpty Dumpty had a great fall.*
*All the King's horses and all the King's*
    *men*
*Couldn't put Humpty Dumpty together*
    *again.*

# Hush-a-Bye, Baby

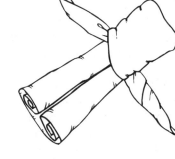

*Hush-a-bye, baby, on the treetop,*
*When the wind blows, the cradle will rock;*
*When the bough bends, the cradle will fall.*
*Down will come baby, cradle and all.*

**T**o reinforce the sound of the letter **H** as in *hush-a-bye*, use cloth handkerchiefs to make these soft dolls.  Children can fold and refold until they learn the technique. Demonstrate each as many times as it takes for the students to learn the steps. When some children learn, they can demonstrate and help other students.

## Hush-a-Bye, Baby

1. Place the handkerchief on a flat surface.  Roll each side to the middle.

2. Fold top half over bottom half.

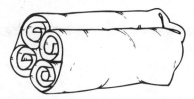

3. Pull the top rolls with care to separate them enough to tie the ends around the doll.  This forms the arms.

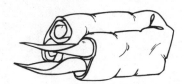

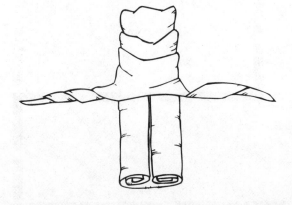

## Baby in a Hammock

1. Fold handkerchief into a triangle.

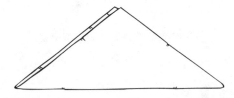

2. Roll right lower corner to middle. Repeat with left side.

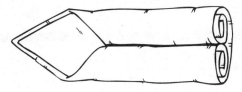

3. Separate top points carefully.

4. Bring back side down under to the opposite side so that the two small rolls appear inside the hammock.

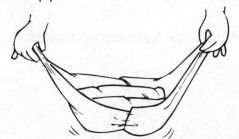

Pattern A

H

# Handful of H Words

**H**ave each child trace her hand in the box below. Round out the bottom of the hand shape as shown. Children are to print as many words that begin with **H** as they can spell or find in books and magazines inside the hand shape.

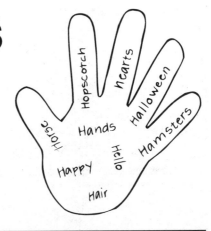

Writing Idea

# H Is for Half

If you divide something into two equal pieces, you have halves. Look at the picture halves for the **H** rhymes below. To make whole pictures, cut out each half on this page and the next page. Paste the matching halves on construction paper. Color each picture. Say the rhymes.

# H Is for Half

# H Is for Harmony

*Hub a dub, dub,*
*Three men in a tub;*
*The butcher, the baker,*
*The candlestick maker.*

**Getting Ready:** Explain to the children that to harmonize means to arrange things in a pleasing way. In music we say certain tones have harmony when they sound good together. In pairs, have the students practice singing the rhyme to the tune of the first two lines of "Twinkle, Twinkle, Little Star." Allow time for the students to practice singing the song to see if their voices harmonize. Let the willing ones share their song. Then play a game to reinforce the concept of harmony.

**Discussion:** Harmony is vanilla ice cream and hot fudge topping. Hot dogs and mustard. Hamburgers and French fries. *Disharmony* is the opposite of *harmony*; it is things that do not belong together. Pickles and ice cream is an example of things that are not harmonious.

**Directions:** Teacher names pairs of food. Children decide if they are harmonious. If they are, they nod their heads up and down. If they are not harmonious, they shake their heads from side to side. See examples below. Then let children name harmonious and disharmonious pairs for the class.

ice cream and dill pickles

apple pie and mustard

toast and jam

popcorn and butter

pancakes and syrup

cheese and crackers

carrots and jelly

candy and bacon

spaghetti and meatballs

coffee and cream

spinach and barbecue sauce

hot dogs and whipped cream

ketchup and chocolate

bread and jam

cauliflower and cookies

tomatoes and cake

macaroni and cheese

bacon and eggs

pasta and chocolate

iced tea and lemon

# Hoagies and Honey Butter

## Honey Butter

Mix 1 cup (240 ml) soft butter or margarine with 1 cup (240 ml) honey. Stir until fluffy. The longer the students stir the honey and butter mixture, the fluffier it will become.

## Hoagies

International

Hoagies are also known as heros, gyros, submarines or grinders. To create a neat classroom treat, buy a loaf or loaves of French bread–enough so that each child can have about a 1" (2.54 cm) taste.

This recipe is for a 12" (30.48 cm) loaf:

½ cup (120 ml) mayonnaise

5 tablespoons (75 ml) mustard

8 slices cheese (American, cheddar, Swiss or other–it's fun to have variety.)

8 slices salami, ham, turkey, bologna or other lunch meats

8 tomato slices

1 cup (240 ml) shredded lettuce

Slice the bread lengthwise. Spread with mayonnaise and mustard. Overlap cheese and meat along the length. If you wish to serve warm, wrap in foil now and heat at 350°F (177°C) for 20 to 30 minutes. Add lettuce and tomato. Slice. Serve. Enjoy!

H

# HOORAY!

_____

knows the shapes of the
uppercase and lowercase **H**.

## Hats Off to You,

because you know the sounds
the letter **H** makes.

**To:** _____

### You Harmonize!

**Y**ou understand harmony.

I'm
so proud
of the
work you have
done with the
letter *H*.

# I i

I sing, I sing,
From morning till night,
From cares I'm free,
And my heart is light.

I had a little hobby horse,
And it was dapple gray,
Its head was made of pea-straw,
Its tail was made of hay.

If all the world were water,
And all the water were ink,
What should we do for bread
 and cheese?
What should we do for drink?

I love you well, my little brother,
And you are fond of me;
Let us be kind to one another,
As brothers ought to be.
You shall learn to play with me,
And learn to use my toys;
And then I think that we shall be
Two happy little boys.

# It's a Round in Two Parts

*I sing, I sing,*
*From morning till night,*
*From cares I'm free,*
*And my heart is light.*

**A** round is a song sung by groups who begin the song at different times. It is a song that harmonizes with itself. The tricky part is singing words that are different from what you hear others sing. It takes concentration! Singing a round is a lot of fun, but you need to make sure that the children know the words to the song. The singers need to concentrate on what they are singing. If they stumble over the words of the song, they will not be able to keep up with the others. Practice singing the rhyme to the tune of the first four lines of "Twinkle, Twinkle, Little Star." Practice and practice. When everyone knows it, try singing it as a round. When the first group begins singing the third line, the second group begins singing the first line. Sing it through as a round three times.

**T**ry using the other two rhymes as speaking rounds. After students know all of the words, break them into two groups. When group one begins the third line, group two begins the first line. Speak in sing-song voices.

*If all the world were water,*
*And all the water were ink,*
*What should we do for bread and*
  *cheese?*
*What should we do for drink?*

*I had a little hobby horse,*
*And it was dapple gray,*
*Its head was made of pea-straw,*
*Its tail was made of hay.*

Ⓘ

# "I Love" Bags

*I love you well, my little brother,*
*And you are fond of me;*
*Let us be kind to one another,*
*As brothers ought to be.*
*You shall learn to play with me,*
*And learn to use my toys;*
*And then I think that we shall be*
*Two happy little boys.*

**D**iscuss the things that the children love the most. Then create felt bags and put heart-shaped paper pictures of these things inside them. To make the bags, you will need scissors; 8" x 8" (20.32 x 20.32 cm) felt; plain paper; pencil; staples; blunt, plastic needle; thread; hole punch; yarn; glue; and beads, buttons or felt cutout decorations.

1. Fold the felt in half and lay the paper pattern so that the flat edge is on the fold of material, and trace around the pattern.

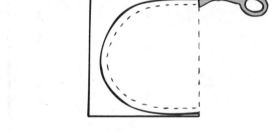

2. Don't unfold the felt. Cut around the edge. Don't cut on the fold. Cut two of these. Unfold and lay flat, one on top of the other.

3. Fold one of the round edges down as illustrated.

4. Staple or stitch around the edges.

5. Punch two holes in the top of the bag. String yarn through the holes to make a handle for the bag.

6. Glue beads, buttons or felt cutout decorations on the bag. Or use markers to decorate it.

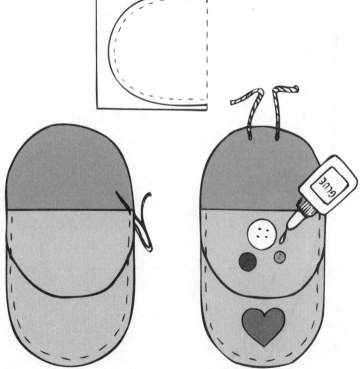

7. Draw pictures of the things that students love the most on heart-shaped paper and put them inside the bags. When children are having a bad day or feel sad, they can look at the pictures in their bags.

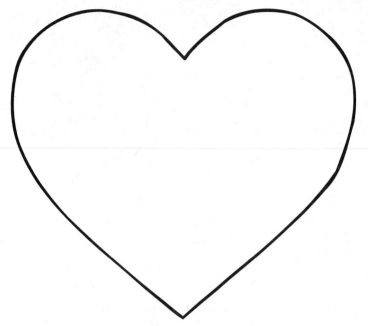
# "I Love" Bags Patterns

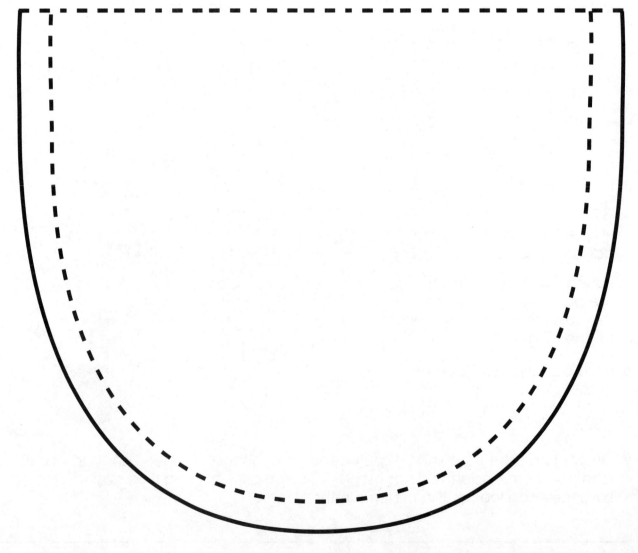

# Life-Sized Is

*I sing, I sing,*
*From morning till night,*
*From cares I'm free,*
*And my heart is light.*

**T**o create a life-sized paper doll of each child, you will need butcher paper, crayons, washable markers or paints, scissors and old clothes that can be cut up. Have each student rest with legs slightly apart and arms out away from the body on a sheet of butcher paper, while another student draws around the outline. Then have students add their own unique facial features and appropriate hair. Let students add clothes to the body shape with crayons, washable markers, paints or cut and paste parts of old clothes on the doll. Yarn can be attached for the hair. When each doll is completed, cut out or have older students help students cut around each outline. Staple to bulletin boards or wall, or use string to hang from the ceiling.

# Pattern Activity

# I Collages

Discuss the idea that a collage is a collection of things that are put together to create a certain impression. Ask the children to think about themselves as a collage. What are the different things that make them who they are? You may want to do a collage of yourself as a sample to show the children. Then give them the pattern for the collage on the next page. Share some of the ideas listed below to get them started.

1. Write your name and decorate it.

2. Cut and paste pictures of your favorite things.

3. Illustrate things that you like to do.

4. Color or paint the collage with your favorite colors.

5. Ask people to write things about you on it.

6. Attach a favorite photograph of yourself.

7. Attach small items that help describe who you are. For example, a baseball card suggests someone who likes baseball.

8. Make a list of some of your favorite things and glue the list to the collage.

9. Draw a picture on the collage or attach a photograph of your favorite place.

10. Write your height, weight, age and physical description on your collage.

I'm 4 feet tall. I have brown hair and brown eyes. I like to fish.

Writing Idea ◇

◇I◇

# Iguana Inches Inside an I

**H**elp the iguana get to the end of the maze. There is only one path through the maze. Can you find it?

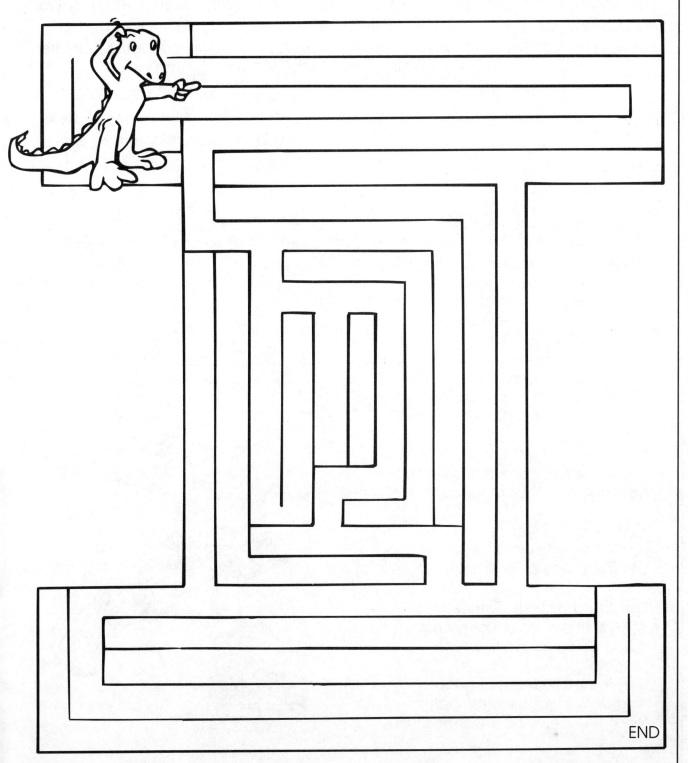

END

*If all the world were water,*
*And all the water were ink,*
*What should we do for bread and cheese?*
*What should we do for drink?*

**Getting Ready:** Say the rhyme with the children. Discuss the word *if*. Then play a game using imaginations.

**Directions:** Say each rhyme below or make up your own, and let the children use their imaginations to fill in the last line. Example:

Teacher asks:

If all the world were <u>ice cream</u>,

And all the water were <u>root beer</u>,

What should we do for <u>dessert</u>?

Children might respond:

We could drink root beer floats.

*If all the rocks were bread,*
*And all the leaves were slices of*
*    cheese,*
*What should we do for supper?*

*If all the world were children,*
*And no one ever grew old,*
*What should we do on birthdays?*

*If all the leaves were dollars,*
*And all the rocks were quarters,*
*Where would we keep all our money?*

*If all the world were Astroturf,*
*And all the stars were floodlights,*
*When could we watch the game?*

*If all the world were feathers,*
*And all the children could fly?*
*How could we get to school?*

*If all the shoes were skates,*
*And all the dirt were ice,*
*What should we do Sunday?*

*If all the days were Saturday,*
*And all the seasons were summer,*
*When could we go to school?*

*If all the world were laughter,*
*And all the water were giggles,*
*What should we do if we sneezed?*

I

# Ice-Cream Dishes

## Frosty and Fiery Bananas
### Bahamas

1. Beat 3 large egg whites until they begin to stiffen. Add 1/4 cup (60 ml) sugar and continue beating until the mixture is stiff.
2. Peel and slice 4 large bananas into halves lengthwise and cut each half into 3 lengths. Arrange half the bananas in a 9" x 13" (22.86 x 33.02 cm) baking dish.
3. Place a 1-pound (45 kg) block of ice cream (well frozen) on top of bananas. Cover with remaining banana slices. Spread with meringue. Bake in 450°F (232°C) oven for 4 minutes or until meringue topping is brown. Serve immediately.

## Ice-Cream Sundaes
### Italy

Have an ice-cream sundae party to celebrate the letter I. Begin by asking each child to describe her favorite ice-cream topping. Make a list on the chalkboard. After everyone has had an opportunity to share, rewrite the list in groups of fruit toppings, nut toppings, etc. Then put the list in sets of different colors or shapes. Vote to see what is the most popular ice-cream topping. You may want to make a large graph on the chalkboard to show the ice-cream topping favorites.

### Ice-Cream Sundae Celebration
Ask everyone to bring in his favorite ice-cream topping. Place scoops of ice cream in deep paper bowls. Assemble all of the toppings on a table. Let each student put the toppings on her own ice cream so everyone can taste several different ones.

### Great Toppings
chopped nuts
fresh fruit
coconut flakes
peanuts
chocolate chips
fudge topping
jams and jellies
whipped topping
banana slices

# I Am *So* Proud!

_____

knows the shapes of the
uppercase and lowercase **I**.

# Incredible!
because you know the sounds
the letter **I** makes.

**To:** _____

## *I Knew You Could Do It!*

**Y**our **I** collage was
irresistible.

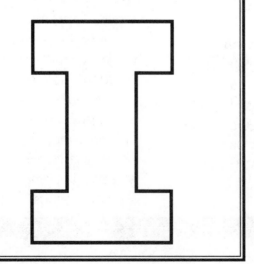

I'm happy
about
your hard
work with the
letter *I*.

# Jj

Jack and Jill went up the hill,
To fetch a pail of water;
Jack fell down and broke his crown,
And Jill came tumbling after.

Handy Spandy, Jack a-dandy,
Loves plum-cake and sugar candy;
He bought some at a grocer's shop,
And out he came, hop-hop-hop.

Jack be nimble; Jack be quick.
Jack jump over the candlestick.

Jack Sprat
Had a cat.
It had but one ear;
It went to buy butter
When butter was dear.

Jack Sprat could eat no fat,
His wife could eat no lean,
And so, between them both, you see,
They licked the platter clean.

# Jazzy Jacks

*Jack Sprat*
*Had a cat.*
*It had but one ear;*
*It went to buy butter*
*When butter was dear.*

Introduce the concept of jazz music to the students. Explain that jazz is a free-form, improvised, unique kind of sound. Jazz is a one-of-a-kind musical happening, often invented as the musician performs. Play some jazz music for the students. Then encourage them to practice singing one of the Jack rhymes in a "jazzy" way.

*Jack and Jill went up the hill,*
*To fetch a pail of water;*
*Jack fell down and broke his crown,*
*And Jill came tumbling after.*

*Jack be nimble; Jack be quick.*
*Jack jump over the candlestick.*

*Jack Sprat could eat no fat,*
*His wife could eat no lean,*
*And so, between them both, you see,*
*They licked the platter clean.*

# J Is for Junk Art

**E**ncourage children to be ecologically minded by using discarded items such as old magazines, oatmeal cartons, coffee tins or paper bags to create beautiful keepsakes.

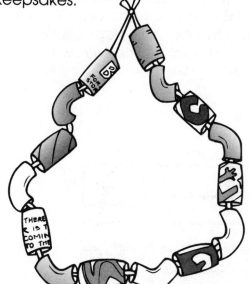

## Paper Bead Necklace

**T**o make paper bead necklaces, children will need old magazines with colorful pages, thin elastic, macaroni, plastic drinking straws, glue and scissors. Cut the colorful magazine pages into 1" x 7" (2.54 x 17.78 cm) strips.

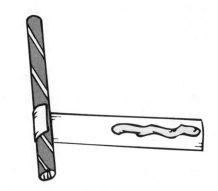

1. Cover half of each strip on one side with glue and place the straw on the unglued end of the strip. Roll up strip on the straw. The glue will hold the paper together.

2. Carefully remove the straw from the bead.

3. When thoroughly dry, alternately string beads and macaroni in an interesting pattern on thin pieces of elastic.

4. When students have enough paper beads and macaroni to make their necklaces as long as they want, tie the elastic in a knot. Encourage students to make several different lengths of necklaces.

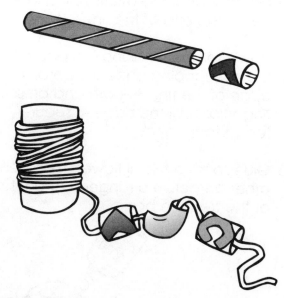

**T**o make a more ornate bead, begin by cutting long thin, triangular pieces instead of strips. Roll up from the wide edge to the point and it will create an interesting shape.

# J Is for Junk Art

## Coffee Tin Treasure Box

To make small treasure boxes, each student will need a small metal box (flavored instant coffee tin), colorful adhesive paper, scissors, ruler and an assortment of dried straw flowers or small shells, etc.

1. Wash and dry the container.

2. Choose an adhesive paper design that you like. Teacher should help students cut a piece about 2¹/₄" x 14" (5.14 x 35.56 cm).

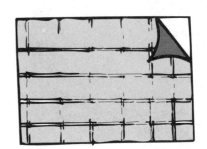

3. Before removing the backing, place paper around the coffee tin and check to make sure the size is exactly what you will need.

4. Lay the adhesive paper on the table and pull off the backing. Place the tin with one end against the edge of the paper so that the overlapping piece will be on the end of the tin.

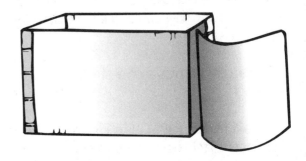

5. Slowly roll the tin along the paper. Press the overlapping paper down along the edge of the tin. Smooth and press with fingertips until the paper is securely fastened to tin.

6. Glue some artificial flowers, seashells or other attractive arrangement on the lid of the treasure box.

# J Is for Junk Art

## Paper Bag Hat

To make a paper bag hat, each student needs a medium or large grocery bag, paint or washable markers, crayons, pieces of yarn, fabric scraps, feathers, artificial or tissue paper flowers, rickrack, paper cutouts, scissors and glue. For younger children, you may want to prepare the bags ahead of time (steps 1 and 2) so students can just do the decorating.

1. Turn the grocery bag inside out. Don't worry about scrunching it, the more the bag is handled, the softer it will become and the better hat it will make. Also, don't worry if the ends of the bag tear slightly, either trim off the tear or assume it will be covered up in the next step.

2. Roll up the ends of the bag to make the brim. How far you roll it up depends on how high you want the crown. A somewhat royal effect can be achieved with a high crown. A low crown will produce a porkpie look or perhaps a beret.

3. Let each student use paints, markers or crayons to decorate the hat. Glue on decorations. Add flowers, a feather or other garnish.

4. Wear and admire!

# J Is for Junk Art

## Oatmeal Carton Bank

To make oatmeal carton banks, each student will need one oatmeal carton. Provide gift wrapping paper, scissors, glue, paintbrush, small bowl, rickrack, sequins, glitter, etc. Prepare the basic bank for students so they can decorate them.

1. Wipe out the inside of the carton. Place lid aside, and then turn the carton upside down.

2. Cut a slit big enough for a half-dollar in the center of the bottom of the carton.

3. In small bowl, mix 1 part glue with 3 parts water. Stir until the glue dissolves in the water.

4. Tear pieces of gift wrap in strips.

5. Apply glue mixture to the outside of carton in a small area. Place a layer of torn paper over the glue. Keep applying glue and paper, overlapping until the whole carton is covered. When you get to the slit, tuck the ends of paper inside the slit.

6. Cover the lid in the same manner.

7. Let dry thoroughly. Replace lid on carton, which will now be the bottom of the bank. To remove money, simply remove the lid from the bottom of bank.

# Jeweled Js

**Directions:** Decorate the uppercase and lowercase **J**s with "jewels" (sequins, synthetic gems, shiny stones, glitter, cellophane cutouts). When thoroughly dry, cut out the letters and attacth them to the cover of your **J** folder. Run your fingers along the edge of each letter. How do they feel?

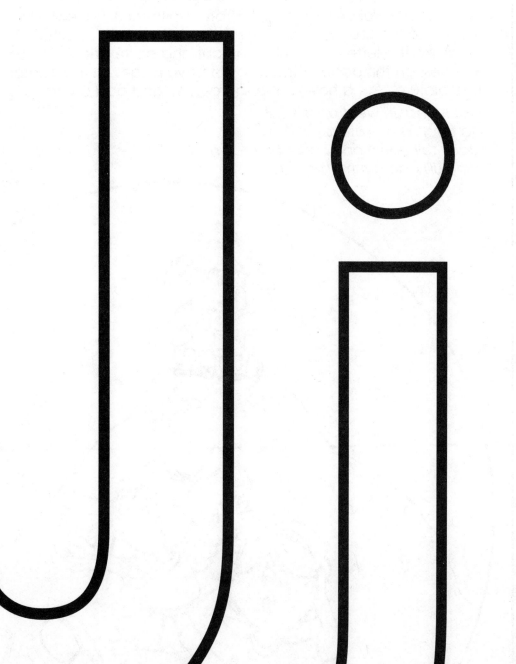

# Writing Idea

# J Wall Plaques

To make a wall plaque to celebrate the letter **J**, have students decorate the edges of a paper plate with the letter **J**. Use paint, washable markers or crayons to make the letters colorful. Then cut and paste one of the scenes of the Jack rhymes, on this page or the following two pages, in the center of the plate. Color the picture. Put a hole at the top center, and add a yarn loop for hanging.

*Jack and Jill went up the hill,*
*To fetch a pail of water;*
*Jack fell down and broke his crown,*
*And Jill came tumbling after.*

126

# J Wall Plaques

*Jack be nimble; Jack be quick.*
*Jack jump over the candlestick.*

**Writing Idea**

*Jack Sprat could eat no fat,*
*His wife could eat no lean,*
*And so, between them both, you see,*
*They licked the platter clean.*

# A Jungle of Js

**H**ow many things that begin with the letter **J** can you find hidden in the jungle? If you look closely you will find a jaguar, jellyfish, jewel, jelly or jam, jack, jack-o'-lantern and a jump rope. Circle each **J** thing and color the picture.

# Jump Rope Games

*Jack be nimble; Jack be quick.*
*Jack jump over the candlestick.*

**Directions:**   Use the Jack rhymes to jump rope.  Jack and Jill might be the easiest to begin with.  Children jump on every underlined word.

Jack and Jill went up the hill,
To fetch a pail of wa/ter;
Jack fell down and broke his crown,
And Jill came tumbling af/ter.

**Variation:**   Hot pepper rope jumping means to pull the rope under the feet twice on one jump. Jump to "Jack Be Nimble" and on the word *candlestick*, try jumping hot peppers.

Jack be nim/ble; Jack be quick.
Jack jump over the candlestick.

**Discussion:**   Explain syncopation to the children.  In syncopation, the off beats are stressed. When you walk, your feet make a regular beat.  When you skip, your feet make a syncopation rhythm.  Jumping rope makes regular rhythms, while Double Dutch rope jumping is an example of syncopation.  For a real challenge, let the students who want to try it, practice syncopation by jumping Double Dutch to every word of "Jack Sprat."  Two people turn two ropes in opposite directions while a third person jumps both ropes.  This will take a great deal of practice.  For the few that can jump Double Dutch, let them practice and demonstrate syncopation jumping for the other students.

| Jack Sprat | could eat | no fat, | |
| His wife | could eat | no lean, | |
| And so, | bet/ween | them both, | you see, |
| They licked | the plat | /ter clean. | |

# Jam and Jelly Js

*Jack Sprat could eat no fat,*
*His wife could eat no lean,*
*And so, between them both, you see,*
*They licked the platter clean.*

## No-Cook Strawberry Jam
### United States

1. Thaw 2 10-ounce (283.5 g) packages of frozen strawberries, or wash and slice 6 boxes of fresh berries. Add 3 1/2 cups (840 ml) sugar. Mix well. Let stand 20 minutes.
2. When sugar has dissolved, add half a 6-ounce (177.44 ml) bottle of liquid fruit pectin. Stir 3 minutes. Ladle into hot, sterilized jars or clean freezer containers. Cover and let stand 24 hours. Seal. Store jam in refrigerator or freezer.

## Grape Jelly
### Germany

1. In a large saucepan, combine 2 cups (480 ml), grape juice concentrate, 2 cups (490 ml) water, juice of 1 lemon, and 1 3/4-ounce (49.61 g) package powdered fruit pectin.
2. Stir over high heat until mixture boils hard. Stir in 4 cups (960 ml) sugar and bring to a full rolling boil; boil hard 1 minute stirring constantly. Remove from heat.
3. Pour into hot, sterilized jelly glasses. Seal at once. Makes 6 jars of jelly.

## J Print Jam Cookies
### England

Use a roll of ready-made sugar cookie dough to make jam press cookies.
1. Give each student a handful of thawed dough. Roll it into a ball and place it on an aluminum-lined cookie sheet. Scratch initials next to each child's cookie.
2. Press the cookie down flat with the palm of the hand. Then instead of just pressing a thumbprint in the top of the cookie, press a letter **J**. Indent the cookie enough so that after it is baked there is plenty of room to fill with jam.

# *Jubilee!*

_____

knows the shapes of the uppercase and lowercase **J**.

# JUST RIGHT!

You know the sounds the letter **J** makes.

**To:** _____

## Jewel Award

**Y**ou made something just beautiful from junk.

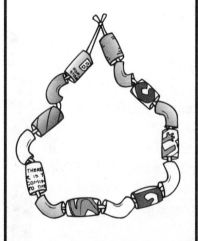

# Jumper Award

You are a terrific rope jumper. You can:

☐    jump rope

☐    jump hot peppers

☐    jump Double Dutch

# Kk

Old King Cole was a merry old soul,
And a merry old soul was he;
And he called for his pipe,
And he called for his bowl,
And he called for his fiddlers three.
And every fiddler, he had a fine fiddle,
And a very fine fiddle had he;
"Tweedle dee, tweedle dee," said the fid-
    dlers:
"Oh, there's none so rare as can compare
With King Cole and his fiddlers three."

K was a kitten,
Who jumped at a cork,
And learned to eat mice
Without plate, knife or fork.

# K Was a Kitten

*K was a kitten,*
*Who jumped at a cork,*
*And learned to eat mice*
*Without plate, knife or fork.*

**C**ut apart the animal alphabet cards. Place them in a hat, bowl or box. The object of this game is for one child to act out one of the animals and for the other children to guess what it is. To play, one child draws a card from the container and hands it to the teacher. The teacher whispers the name on the card to the child and makes sure the child is familiar with the animal. The child pantomimes or acts out the animal for the other students. (You may wish to make this a true charade, or you might want to allow sound effects.) With very young children, it is probably a good idea to review all the animals and talk about them. Some children may not be familiar with all the animals or their names. If you feel that some are too obscure for your students, you may wish to remove those cards from the game. For older children who are reading, it may be helpful to write all the animal names on the board so that students may refer to them during the game. Give students 20 to 30 seconds to guess. The game can also be played in teams.

| Ape | Newt |
|-----|------|
| Bat | Ostrich |
| Cow | Penguin |
| Dog | Quail |
| Elephant | Rooster |
| Fox | Spider |
| Goat | Turkey |
| Hamster | Uakaris |
| Inchworm | Vulture |
| Jackrabbit | Woodpecker |
| Kitten | X-ray fish |
| Lion | Yak |
| Mouse | Zebra |

# Kaleidoscope of Ks

One way to reinforce the letter **K** is to make sponge stamp print patterns in a kaleidoscope of colors. For this project you will need new household sponges, paper, tempera paint, fine-tip washable markers, scissors and paper plates.

1. Provide each student with patterns for the letter **K** on the next page. Prepare the K stamps ahead of time. Place pattern on a sponge, use a marker to trace around the pattern.

2. Cut out the sponge letter.

3. Wet the sponge stamps with water and squeeze out excess water so they are pliable.

4. Place a different color of tempera paint in each paper plate. Children create a kaleidoscope of **K**s by dipping the sponge stamp into the paint and stamping the paper in a kaleidoscope of colors.

5. When changing colors of paint, students should wash out the sponge stamp and squeeze out excess water.

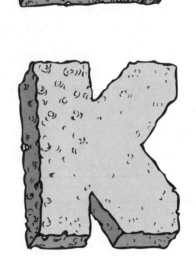

# Kaleidoscope of Ks Patterns

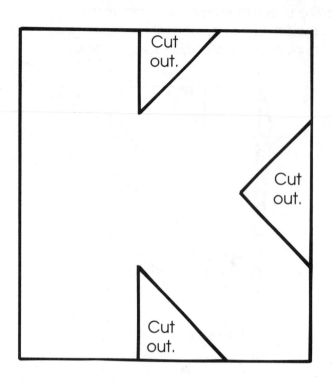

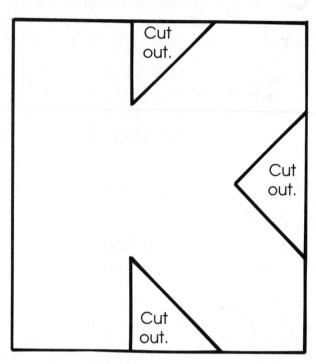

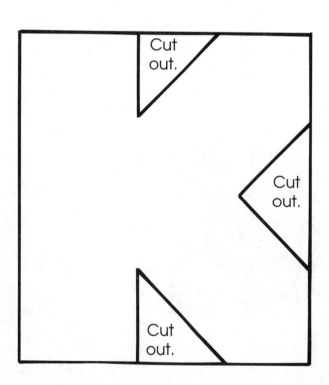

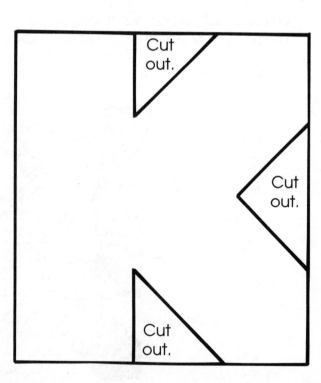

# Ks Are Key

**Directions:** Use the key pattern to decorate the uppercase and lowercase Ks. Trace the outline of the key onto the paper Ks. Color with gold and silver crayons or washable markers. Cut out the letters and attach them to the cover of your **K** folder.

# K Knots

**C**ut an 8" (20.32 cm) and a 12" (30.48 cm) piece of yarn. Tie the pieces in the middle as shown. Then spread them out to look like the letter **K**. Long ends are the legs. Glue the knotted **K** in the box below. When dry, run your fingers on the letter. Can you make a lowercase **K** with knotted yarn? Try it.

# What's That K Thing?

On this page and the following page, cut out and paste the correct word under each picture. Color the pictures.

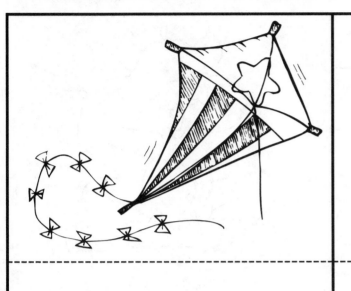

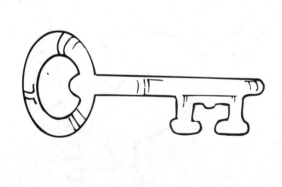

| ketchup | King Cole |
|---------|-----------|
| kitten  | kite      |

# What's That K Thing?

**O**n this page and the preceding page, cut out the **K** picture cards, color and use as flash cards.

GRANDMA'S KITCHEN

Ketchup

| koala | key |
|-------|-----|
| kangaroo | kitchen |

K

# Tied in Knots

**Getting Ready:** Choose a sunny day for this out-of-doors game. It should be a day when the grass is dry because the children may end up on the grass during the game.

**Directions:** Divide children into groups of 3 or 4. Each group of children stands in a small circle. Each child takes hold of another child's hand. With the other hand he takes hold of a different child's hand. The idea is to make a knot of all the arms and hands in the middle of the circle. Then without letting go of hands, the children duck and move around and try to untie the knot of arms. It may not be possible to completely untie the tangled mess. How close can they get? Have fun with this.

**Variation 1:** For a race, have two or three groups trying to untie themselves at the same time.

**Variation 2:** Play the game with one person as the communicator who gives verbal directions to the members of the group.

**Variation 3:** Play the game with the rule that no one can speak.

**Discussion:** Talk about whether it was easier to untie the knot when there was one person in charge of the group and talking was allowed.

K

# Kebabs

The students can make kebabs stacked with cooked meats, cheeses, vegetables and fruits. Ask each child to bring 1 to 2 cups (240 to 480 ml) of his favorite lunch meat, cheese, raw vegetables or fruit cut into 1" (2.54 cm) cubes or bite-sized chunks. Make a list on the board of food possibilities. Examples:

| | |
|---|---|
| **American cheese** | **celery** |
| **Swiss cheese** | **green peppers** |
| **cheddar cheese** | **cherry tomatoes** |
| **ham** | **apples** |
| **salami** | **bananas** |
| **shrimp** | **pineapple** |
| **cauliflower** | **cherries** |
| **carrots** | **grapes** |

### Kebabs

On serving day, have the students place all the different foods on paper plates. Group the meats, cheeses, vegetables and fruits in sets and arrange on a table. Set out colored toothpicks, thin drinking straws or coffee stir sticks and small paper plates. Serve with crackers and breadsticks. After the food is assembled, but before anyone begins to construct her kebab, hold a class discussion.

**Discussion:** What foods could we use to make an all red and yellow kebab? Can someone name the kinds of lunch meats on the table? What shape is the cheese? What color are the breadsticks? How many different kinds of apples do we have? Count the vegetables, etc.

# Kebabs

### Chicken Kebabs
Pakistan

Open-air cooking of kebabs can be traced back for centuries to Russia where meat was cooked on swords and roasted over an open fire. You can cook chicken kebab on a barbeque or use a rotisserie in an oven.

1. Place 1 pound (45 kg) peeled and chopped onions, 4 cloves of crushed garlic, 3 crushed cardamom seeds, 1 tablespoon (15 ml) chili powder and 1 teaspoon (5 ml) salt into bowl and mix into a paste. Add a few drops of water if you need it to get a paste consistency.
2. Rub mixture into the chicken and leave for half an hour. If any of the paste slips off, rub it back into the chicken.
3. Melt ½ cup (120 ml) butter for basting chicken.
4. Place chicken on skewer and grill over charcoal or in the rotisserie. Baste with butter every few minutes. Cook slowly until the chicken is tender.

### Kebabs with Peanut Sauce
Malaysia and Indonesia

When serving this dish, make the sauce first.

1. Grind 1 cup (240 ml) skinned peanuts into a paste. Add 2 teaspoons (10 ml) water and 1 teaspoon (5 ml) sugar to peanut paste. Finely chop 2 tablespoons (30 ml) onion and add a clove of crushed garlic. Mix into peanut paste.
2. Cut meat (fish, chicken, beef or lamb) into small cubes about 1" (2.54 cm) square and rub each with peanut paste.
3. Thread each piece onto a small skewer and rub each piece with peanut oil. Grill, turning frequently.
4. While meat is cooking, add 1 cup (240 ml) cream to remaining peanut paste and stir until smooth. Warm slightly. When meat is brown, serve on the sticks with the sauce in a separate bowl for dipping.

## You Know

the shapes of the
uppercase and lowercase **K**.

_____

## Keen!

because you know the sounds
the letter **K** makes.

**To:** _____

## Outstanding!

**Y**ou can read these
words that begin with **K**.

☐ kitten          ☐ key
☐ kangaroo    ☐ kitchen
☐ koala         ☐ ketchup
☐ kite            ☐ King Cole

Great work with K!

# Ll

**L**ittle Jack Horner
Sat in a corner,
Eating a Christmas pie;
He put in his thumb,
And pulled out a plum,
And said, "What a good boy am I!"

**L**ittle-Bo-Peep has lost her sheep,
And can't tell where to find them;
Let them alone, and they'll come home,
And bring their tails behind them.

**L**adybug, Ladybug, fly away home.
Your house is on fire, your children all gone,
All but one, and her name is Ann,
And she crept under the pudding pan.

**L**ittle boy blue, come blow your horn;
The sheep's in the meadow; the cow's in the corn.
Where's the little boy that looks after the sheep?
He's under the hay-stack, fast a-sleep.

# Let's Create New Lyrics

*Little Jack Horner*
*Sat in a corner,*
*Eating a Christmas pie;*
*He put in his thumb,*
*And pulled out a plum,*
*And said, "What a good boy am I!"*

**E**xplain to the children that lyrics are words set to music. Matching the number of notes to the number of syllables is the important thing to remember when writing lyrics. Sometimes lyrics rhyme, but they don't always have to. One easy way to have children create lyrics is to change words in a familiar poem or song.

**Example:**
Little Lynn Willow
Sat on a pillow,
Eating a lemon cake;
She put in her thumb,
And pulled out some gum,
And said, "What a great big mistake."

In small groups, have the children make up new lyrics for an **L** rhyme.

*Little-Bo-Peep has lost her sheep,*
*And can't tell where to find them;*
*Let them alone, and they'll come home,*
*And bring their tails behind them.*

*Little boy blue, come blow your horn;*
*The sheep's in the meadow; the cow's in the corn.*
*Where's the little boy that looks after the sheep?*
*He's under the hay-stack, fast a-sleep.*

L

# L Links

**U**se the lowercase **L** pattern below to make paper links. Pre-cut them for the children. Make them in a variety of colors. Pre-cut the other link patterns, too. Be sure to cut them double with the fold across the dotted edge. Link the **L**s by gluing the ends together. Link the other pieces by putting one inside the other. Demonstrate both methods of making paper chains. If children wish, both ends of a chain of links can be attached to each other to make paper link leis. When discussing the links, use adjectives that begin with the letter **L**.

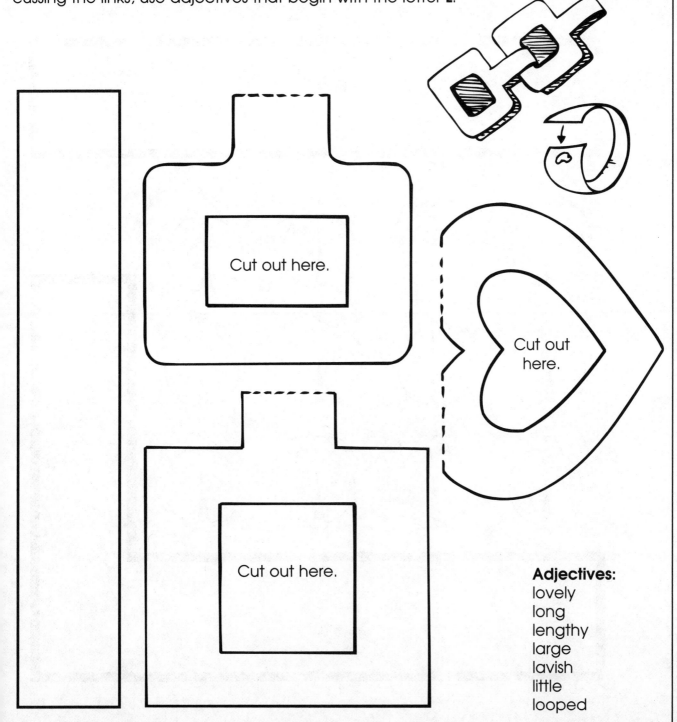

**Adjectives:**
lovely
long
lengthy
large
lavish
little
looped

# Ladybug Ls

**Directions:** Cut out the ladybugs below and paste them on the uppercase and lowercase **L**s. Color each ladybug with a red crayon. Then use a hole punch and black construction paper to make little ladybug spots. Glue them on the ladybug's back. When dry, cut out the letters and glue them on the cover of your **L** folder. Run your fingers over each letter. How do the dots on the bugs feel? How do the edges of the letters feel? (If the black dots are too small for your children to handle, they can use black crayons or markers to draw on the spots.)

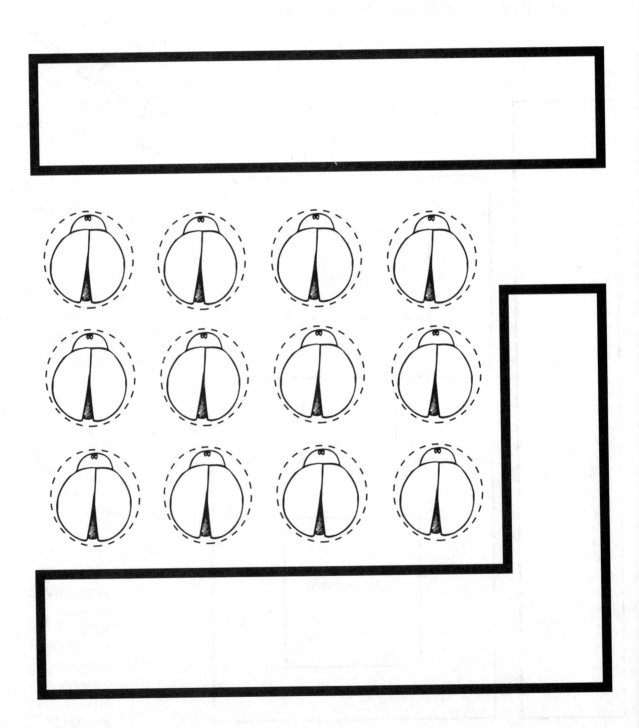

L

# Lovely Literature

Use some of the stamps of **L** words on this page to complete the rebus story on the next two pages. Cut out each stamp. Glue the ones you choose in the story. The stamps you choose to use will make your story different from everyone else's story. You will not need every stamp. Just use the ones you like best.

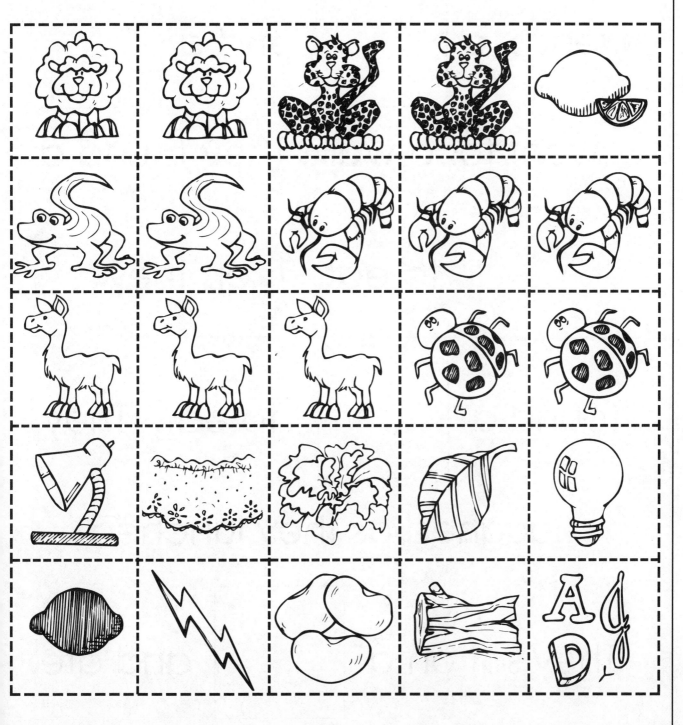

LI

**Writing Idea**

# Lovely Literature

Once upon a time, two

friends, a  and a  ,

went for a walk. They found a

 to eat.  Then they

found a  to eat.  They

laughed as they lunched.

They sat on a  and ate.

# Lovely Literature

Then a  saw the

two friends eating. "How

can you eat those things?"

it asked. "I like ."

The two friends shook

their heads and smiled,

"We like this lunch."

# Sorting Out L Things

**S**ort out the **L** things. Begin by cutting out the things that begin with **L** and color them. On the next page, paste the foods in the lunch pail. Paste the animals in the cage. Paste the tools in the box.

# Sorting Out L Things

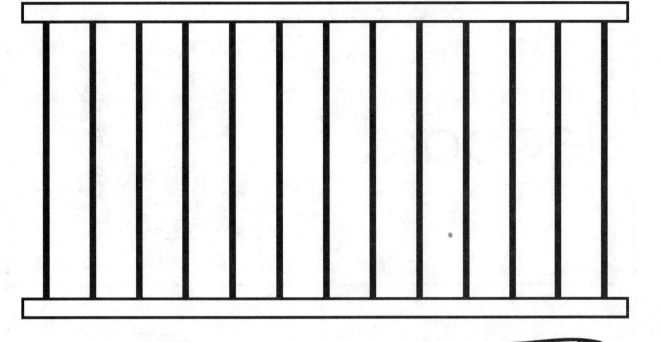

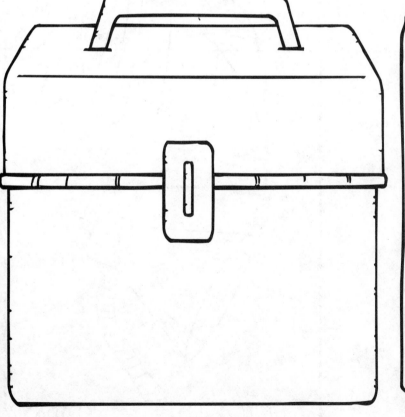

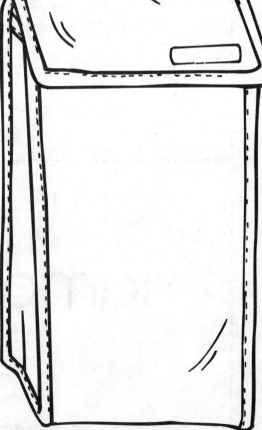

# Look and Concentrate

**Getting Ready:** Reproduce cards on this page and the following two pages on light cardboard or heavy paper. Give each student his own set of cards to color and cut apart.

leopard

leaf

lamp

**Directions:** Shuffle cards. Lay them facedown. Take turns turning over two cards at a time. If the picture and word match, player keeps the cards. If they do not match, player turns them facedown again. Continue playing until all of the cards have been collected.

# ladybug

# log

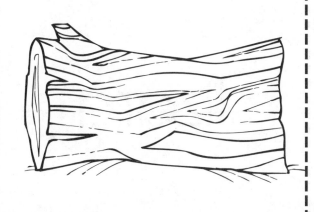

# lion

**L**

**Variation:** Students can use the picture and word cards to play a matching game or to make a booklet of pictures and words. To make a book, don't cut pictures and words apart. Assemble pages in any order.

lamb

lizard

lobster

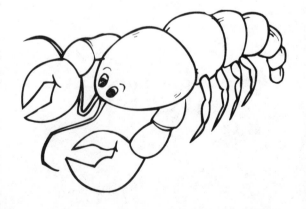

# Luscious L Lunch

### Lacy Lettuce Roll-Ups
Germany

Wash and dry iceberg lettuce leaves. Spread each one with soft cream cheese and place a thin slice of ham or dried beef on each. Roll up.

### Lentil Soup
Britain

1. Wash 1 pound (.45 kg) of lentils thoroughly and put in a large saucepan or slow cooker.
2. Add 7 cups (1680 ml) water and 1 ham bone. Stir. Put 1 bay leaf, 2 cloves of garlic and salt and pepper in lentils. Bring to a gentle boil; cook over low heat for 1 to 2 hours until lentils are mushy. Cook longer if using a slow cooker.
3. When lentils are cooked, remove bay leaf and ham bone. Mash lentils and stir until smooth. Return to heat and add 2 cups (480 ml) cream. Warm again. Serve immediately.

### Lime Soup
Mexico

1. Shred 2 cold, cooked chicken breasts.
2. Saute 1 thinly sliced onion, 1 finely chopped green pepper, 3 cloves of minced garlic and 2 medium tomatoes peeled and chopped. Add to the cooked vegetables the juice of 1 lime. Stir this mixture into 2 quarts (1.91 l) of chicken broth and bring to a boil. Add shredded chicken. Heat. Serve with tortilla chips.

### Lemon Lady Fingers
Germany

Use frozen cookie dough and a can of prepared lemon icing to make quick and easy lady fingers.
1. Give each child a small handful of dough. Roll the dough into lowercase **L** shapes. Place on aluminum-lined baking sheet. Mark cookies by scratching initials in aluminum foil next to each cookie. Bake as directed on package.
2. When cool, frost with lemon icing.

# *Lovely!*

_____

knows the shapes of the uppercase and lowercase **L**.

# Listen Up!

You know the sounds the letter **L** makes.

**To:** _____

# OUTSTANDING!

**Y**ou can read these animal words that begin with **L**.

☐ lion     ☐ leopard

☐ ladybug     ☐ lobster

☐ lizard     ☐ lamb

**I'm so proud of the work you have done with the letter *L*.**

# Mm

**M**ary, Mary, quite contrary,
How does your garden grow?
With silver bells and cockle shells,
And pretty maids all in a row.

**M**ary had a little lamb
With fleece as white as snow,
And everywhere that Mary went
The lamb was sure to go.

It followed her to school one day,
That was against the rule;
It made the children laugh and play,
To see a lamb at school.

And so the teacher turned it out,
But still it lingered near,
And waited patiently about
Till Mary did appear.

"Why does the lamb love Mary so?"
The eager children cry.
"Why, Mary loves the lamb, you know!"
The teacher did reply.

# Mary Had a Little Monkey

*Mary had a little lamb
With fleece as white as snow,
And everywhere that Mary went
The lamb was sure to go.*

*It followed her to school one day,
That was against the rule;
It made the children laugh and play,
To see a lamb at school.*

**P**ractice singing the first two original verses. Then sing and substitute **M** animals for *lamb*. When singing these new verses, you may choose to use the masks on pages 166-168.

Mary had a little monkey
With fur as white as snow,
And everywhere that Mary went
The monkey was sure to go.

It followed her to school one day,
That was against the rule;
It made the children laugh and play,
To see a monkey at school.

Mary had a musical moose;
It could sing and dance, you know,
And everywhere that Mary went
The moose was sure to go.

It followed her to school one day,
That was against the rule;
It made the children laugh and play,
To see a moose at school.

Mary had a giant mule.
It wore a big blue bow,
And everywhere that Mary went
The mule was sure to go.

It followed her to school one day,
That was against the rule;
It made the children laugh and play,
To see a mule at school.

# Marvelous, A"maze"ing Ms

*Mary, Mary, quite contrary,*
*How does your garden grow?*
*With silver bells and cockle shells,*
*And pretty maids all in a row.*

To create an amazing **M** that is fun and easy, you will need to have paper, pencil and crayons for each student. Children begin by drawing an uppercase or lower-case **M** in the center of their papers. Close the bottom of the letter with a line and use one color to fill inside the letter. Next, draw around the outside of the let-ter, repeating the shape until the paper is filled. Encourage students to make some lines thicker and use a variety of colors.

After this technique is mastered, children may want to use a bell shape or shell shape in the center to illustrate the rhyme.

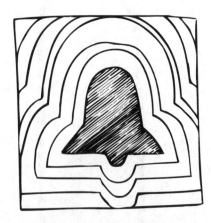 

Pattern Activity

M

M

m

TLC10000 Copyright © Teaching & Learning Company, Carthage, IL 62321

# Straw M Sculptures

**F**lex straws are perfect for creating three-dimensional **M**s. Bend one straw and hold the short side down to make one half of the letter as illustrated. Bend another straw to make the other half. Help children glue straws to create an abstract three-dimensional design of many letter **M**s. Straw sculptures can overlap each other and should be placed randomly on the page. Glue each straw on the paper and let dry. When dry, outline **M** shapes with different colors of washable markers or crayons.

**Variation:** Instead of drawing around the **M**s with crayons or washable markers, outline the edges of each letter with yarn and glue in place.

Writing Idea

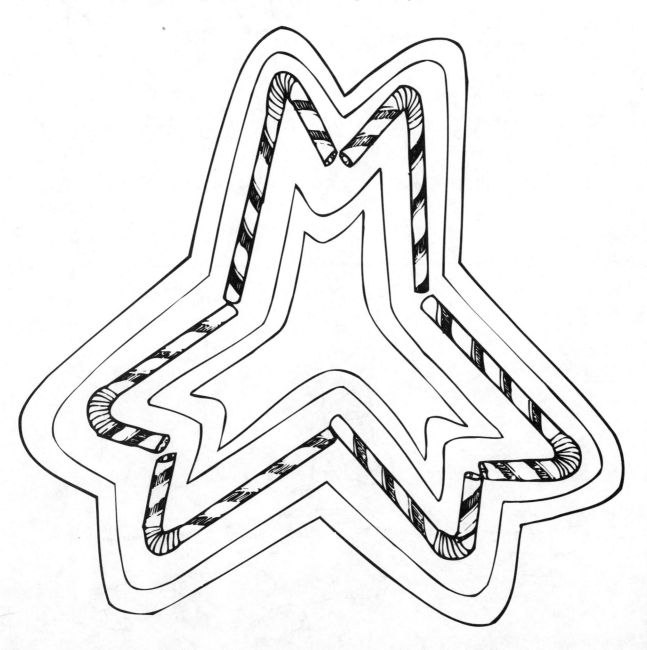

# What's Missing?

**D**raw the monkey's mouth, the alligator's arm, the cat's tail and the elephant's eye. Color the animals.

# Masks and Mimics

**Getting Ready:** To play this game students will need to make one of the **M** animal masks. Patterns are on pages 166-168. Use the new version of "Mary Had a Little Lamb" on page 160.

**Directions:** Children sit in a circle with mask on the floor in front of them. One student holds up his mask, and the children sing the appropriate verse of the song.

**Example:** A student holds up the mule mask, everyone sings the mule version of the rhyme. Continue moving around the circle holding up different masks and singing different verses. Or all the mules can sing a verse about mules, etc.

**How to Make the Masks:**

1. Cut two slits (about 2" (5.08 cm) long) on each side of a 10" (25.4 cm) paper plate as illustrated.

2. Staple and tape a tongue depressor or craft stick to the inside of the plate at the bottom as illustrated.

3. Cut out an **M** animal face (see patterns on pages 166-168). Turn the plate over and glue on the face. Use crayons and markers to decorate the mask.

4. Help each student cut tiny peep holes in her mask so she can see from behind.

5. Overlap each slit and staple closed. The plate will bend out giving a 3-D effect.

**Variation:** Play a guessing game. One student goes to the center of the circle and moves in a particular way to mimic an **M** animal while the other students guess. When someone guesses correctly, everyone sings the appropriate verse as the student in the center continues to move and mimic his chosen **M** animal.

# Masks and Mimics Patterns
## Monkey

# Masks and Mimics Patterns
## Mule

# Masks and Mimics Patterns

## Moose

# Molding Marvelous Marzipan

*Mary, Mary, quite contrary,*
*How does your garden grow?*
*With silver bells and cockle shells,*
*And pretty maids all in a row.*

**M**arzipan is a no-cook, almond candy usually formed in the shapes of fruits and vegetables. Below are two different recipes for creating marzipan that the children can use to mold into bells and shells or **M** shapes such as moons, mushrooms, muffins, meatballs, melons, etc. Encourage them to think of their own **M** shapes to mold.

## Marzipan Fruit Paste
### Italy

1. Mix 2 cups (480 ml) almond paste, 2 cups (480 ml) confectioners' sugar, 3 egg whites, 2 tablespoons (30 ml) white corn syrup and 1 teaspoon (5 ml) almond extract together until a smooth, stiff paste is obtained. Or mix in a blender at low speed.
2. Keep paste mixture in a covered jar to prevent hardening. Use a drop of food coloring to make paste different colors.
3. Give each child a spoonful of paste to mold. Chill until dry.

## Quick and Easy Marzipan
### United States

Use a blender or food processor to mix 2 cups (480 ml) coconut flakes, 1 package (3 oz. [85 g]) flavored gelatin, 1 cup (240 ml) ground almonds or almond paste, 2/3 cup (160 ml) sweetened condensed milk, 1 teaspoon (5 ml) sugar and 1 teaspoon (5 ml) almond extract together until a stiff paste is formed. Keep paste mixture in a covered jar to prevent hardening. After molding into desired shapes, chill until dry.

# Monumental!

_____

knows the shapes of the uppercase and lowercase **M**.

# Marvelous!

You know the sounds the letter **M** makes.

**To:** _____

# A "maze"ing You!

**Y**ou made a marvelous **M** mask.

**Mmmmmm,** I'm proud of the work you did with the letter **M**.

# Nn

**N**ose, nose, jolly red nose;
And what gave you that jolly red nose?
Nutmeg and cinnamon, spices and cloves,
They gave me this jolly red nose.

**T**he nightingale sings when we're at rest;
The nightingale sings when we're at rest;
The little bird climbs the tree for his nest,
With a hop, step and a jump.

**T**he North Wind doth blow.
We soon shall have snow,
And what will the robin do then?
   Poor thing.
He'll sit in a barn,
And keep himself warm,
And hide his head under his wing.
   Poor thing.

**N** was a nosegay,
Sprinkled with dew,
Pulled in the morning
And presented to you.

**Nn**

**Circle Time**

# Sing a Nightingale's Song

*The nightingale sings when we're at rest;*
*The nightingale sings when we're at rest;*
*The little bird climbs the tree for his nest,*
*With a hop, step and a jump.*

**T**urn the rhyme into a group participation song with the sounds and actions below. Assign speaking parts to individuals or small groups. Every time a certain word is spoken, the individual or group makes the appropriate sound. Then have the children recite the rhyme while participating in it.

*nightingale*  (tweedy dee, tweedy dee)
*sings*        (tweet, tweet)
*rest*         (snoring sounds)
*bird*         (chirp, chirp)
*tree*         (swish, swish)

**E**veryone does the hop, step and jump.

**U**se actions to learn this rhyme:

| | |
|---|---|
| *The North Wind doth blow,* | (Wrap arms around body.) |
| *We soon shall have snow,* | (Wiggle fingers overhead like snow.) |
| *And what will the robin do then?* | (Shrug shoulders, shake head slowly.) |
| *Poor thing.* | (Sigh!) |
| *He'll sit in a barn,* | (Form barn roof with hands overhead.) |
| *And keep himself warm,* | (Wrap arms around body.) |
| *And hide his head under his wing.* | (Put head under one arm.) |
| *Poor thing.* | (Sigh!) |

172

# Papier-Mâché Ns

*N was a nosegay,
Sprinkled with dew,
Pulled in the morning
And presented to you.*

It is easy for children to make papier-mâché **N**s. You will need to have all supplies available. You may want to complete steps 1-4 for each student.

1. Roll an 8¹/₂" x 11" (21.6 x 27.94 cm) piece of paper.

2. Divide it into three equal parts and bend it to make an **N**. This is the base. Place it on several layers of newspaper.

3. Rip newspaper into strips about 1" (2.54 cm) wide.

4. Mix ¹/₂ cup (120 ml) flour with 1 tablespoon (15 ml) salt and 1 cup (240 ml) warm water to make a runny paste.

5. Students dip the newpaper strips into the paste and layer them over the **N**. Wrap around all the edges. Make sure the letters will stand up on their own.

6. When the papier-mâché is dry and ready to paint, it will feel hard to the touch. A day is usually long enough to dry small papier-mâché objects.

7. When completely dry, paint and decorate with markers, glitter, stickers, etc.

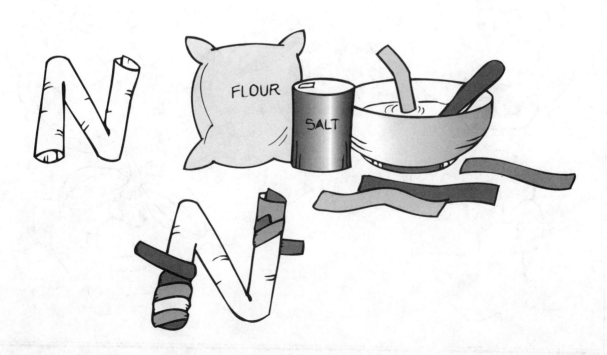

# A New Nose

*Nose, nose, jolly red nose;*
*And what gave you that jolly red nose?*
*Nutmeg and cinnamon, spices and cloves,*
*And they gave me this jolly red nose.*

**T**o celebrate the sound of **N** as in *nose* and the sense of smell, conduct a discussion about noses and create a classroom bulletin board. Begin by covering the board with white paper. With a washable, black marker, write a title and the nose rhyme on the board. Children are to cut out large faces and noses from old magazines. Paste a new nose on each face and attach to the board. Try to cover the board with a collage of faces. Discuss how different people look with new noses. Examine all of the noses on the bulletin board and let the class choose the funniest nose, most interesting nose, most beautiful nose, largest nose, tiniest nose, etc. Discuss the sense of smell. Find out what aroma children enjoy smelling the most. Create a class list of favorite smells. Who likes the smell of gasoline? Bread baking? Hard-boiled eggs? Lemons? Burning rubber? Skunks? Wet dogs? Roses?

### No News Is Good News

Nose, nose, jolly red nose;
And what gave you that jolly red nose?
Nutmeg and cinnamon, spices and cloves,
And they gave me this jolly red nose.

# Noodle Ns

**Directions:** Egg noodles boiled with a few drops of food coloring in the water make an interesting craft material. While still moist, place cooked noodles on both the uppercase and lowercase **N**s. Place students' work on several sheets of newspaper and leave to dry for several days. When thoroughly dry, cut out the letters and attach them to the cover of your **N** folder. How do the noodles feel? Run your fingers over the edges of the letters.

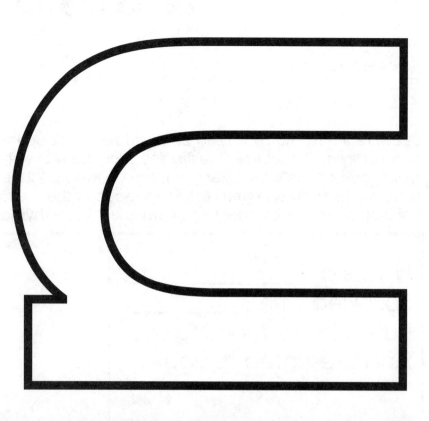

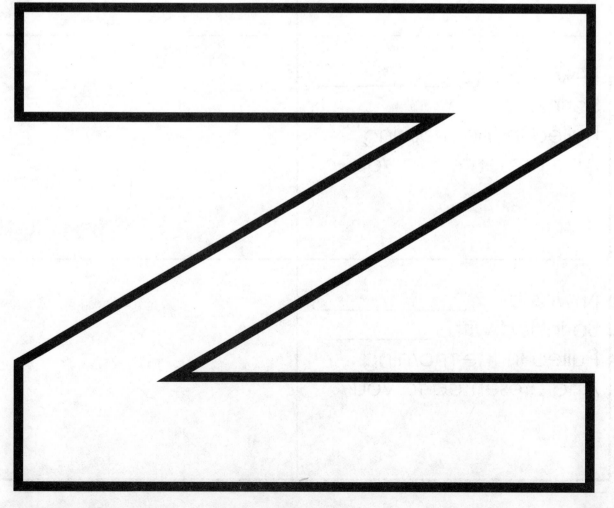

## Writing Idea

# N Was a Nosegay

*N was a nosegay,*
*Sprinkled with dew,*
*Pulled in the morning*
*And presented to you.*

**R**ewrite the rhyme by having each student replace the last word in the first and second lines. The word in the first line should begin with an **N**. As students dictate new words for the rhyme, record them on the worksheet. Do it three times. Then have students draw a little picture for each of the rhymes. When finished, have children put a star by their favorite rhyme. Share rhymes with the class.

| | |
|---|---|
| N was a _____,<br>Sprinkled with _____,<br>Pulled in the morning<br>And presented to you. | |
| N was a _____,<br>Sprinkled with _____,<br>Pulled in the morning<br>And presented to you. | |
| N was a _____,<br>Sprinkled with _____,<br>Pulled in the morning<br>And presented to you. | |

# North Wind Doth Blow

*The North Wind doth blow.*
*We soon shall have snow,*
*And what will the robin do then?*

**P**oor Robin keeps warm by hopping to a barn.  Where do other animals keep warm in the winter?  Draw a line to match each animal with its home.  Color the animals and their homes.

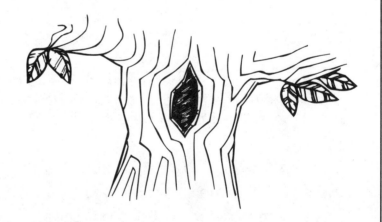

# The Nose Knows

*Nose, nose, jolly red nose;*
*And what gave you that jolly red nose?*
*Nutmeg and cinnamon, spices and cloves,*
*And they gave me this jolly red nose.*

**Getting Ready:** Discuss noses. Talk about how we only have one and it sticks out right in the middle of our face! It can smell aromas and make eating food more enjoyable. It filters the air that we breath.

**Directions:** Teach the children the following rhyme. Then recite it as they touch each part of their face as indicated.

| | |
|---|---|
| *Brow brinky* | (eyebrow) |
| *Eye winky* | (eyelid) |
| *Chin choppy* | (chin) |
| *Nose noppy* | (nose) |
| *Cheek cherry* | (cheek) |
| *Mouth merry.* | (lips) |

**Variation:** Here is another nursery rhyme to celebrate the face. You might choose to read the rhyme to the class and have them guess what part of the face each line of the rhyme is about before actions are used.

| | |
|---|---|
| *Here sits the Lord Mayor* | (forehead) |
| *Here sit his two men.* | (eyes) |
| *Here sits the rooster* | (right cheek) |
| *Here sits the hen* | (left cheek) |
| *Here sit the little chickens* | (top of nose) |
| *Here they run in* | (mouth) |
| *Chinchopper, chinchopper,* | |
| *Chinchopper, chin!* | (chin) |

# N Is for Noodles

## Cold Noodles

Japan

1. Cook 1 pound (.45 kg) vermicelli noodles until tender.
2. Drain and rinse under cold running water. Chill.
3. Heat 1 cup (240 ml) chicken broth and 1/4 cup (60 ml) soy sauce in a small saucepan and simmer 5 minutes. Cool and chill.
4. Pour sauce over noodles, sprinkle with ginger and scallions. Mix. Serve noodles in small individual bowls.

## Cold Noodles with Sesame Seeds

Taiwan

In Taiwan, cold noodles are bought and eaten in the streets. Layers of different ingredients are spooned separately over the cold, cooked noodles and the buyer mixes it himself.
1. Cook 1 pound (.45 kg) of ramen noodles (Chinese style) in plenty of fast boiling water for about 5 minutes or until noodles are tender. Drain. Rinse well in cold water and drain again. Chill.
2. Before serving, sprinkle with sesame seeds, chopped peanuts or other toppings of your choice.

## Green Noodles with Cheese

Italy

1. Bring a large pot of water to a rolling boil. Add a pinch of salt and a 12 oz. (340.2 kg) bag of green spinach noodles. Cook until tender. Drain well and return to the pot.
2. Add 2 tablespoons (30 ml) butter and 2 cups (480 ml) tomato sauce.
3. Grate 1/2 cup (120 ml) Parmesan cheese and sprinkle on top. Bake at 350°F (177°C) until top is golden, about 10 minutes.

## Fried Noodles

China

A classic and yet simple Chinese dish is stir-fried noodles served with whatever meat, seafood and green vegetables are available. Noodles have to be parboiled before they are fried.
1. Bring a large pan of water to a rolling boil and put in noodles. Cook until tender. Drain well.
2. Stir-fry noodles with chicken strips, chunks of fish or vegetables.

N

## NICE!

_____

knows the shapes of the
uppercase and lowercase **N**.

## News Bulletin!

You know the sounds of the letter **N**.

**To:**_____

## GREAT WORK

with the letter **N**.

**For:** _____

## Neat!

_____

knows how to rewrite
an **N** rhyme.

# Oo

Old Mother Goose, when
She wanted to wander,
Would ride through the air
On a very fine gander.

Old Mother Hubbard
Went to the cupboard
To get her poor dog a bone.
But when she came there
The cupboard was bare,
And so the poor dog had none.

There was an old woman who lived in a shoe,
She had so many children, she didn't know what to do.
She gave them some broth, without any bread,
She whipped them all 'round, and sent them to bed.

# Old Mother's Sing-Along

*Old Mother Goose, when she wanted to wander,*
*Would ride through the air on a very fine gander.*

**Y**ou might try singing "There Was an Old Woman" to the tune of "On Top of Old Smoky." "Old Mother Goose" to the tune of "Here We Go 'Round the Mulberry Bush" and "Old Mother Hubbard" to the tune of "Are You Sleeping, Brother John?" The words do not fit exactly, but children can improvise a bit or make up new tunes. Practice singing all three rhymes. Then perform them for another class.

*There was an old woman who lived in a shoe,*
*She had so many children, she didn't know what to do.*
*She gave them some broth, without any bread,*
*She whipped them all 'round, and sent them to bed.*

*Old Mother Hubbard*
*Went to the cupboard*
*To get her poor dog a bone.*
*But when she came there*
*The cupboard was bare,*
*And so the poor dog had none.*

# Old Mother Hubbard's Cupboard Band

Use things found in the kitchen cupboard to make musical instruments. After students create instruments, have them use their instruments to accompany the rhyme.

### Spoon Timekeepers

Tap the rounded part of two tablespoons together in time to music. Try tapping the handles together for a different sound. Tie the spoons together with a bit of yarn at the base of the rounded part of the spoon to make castanets.

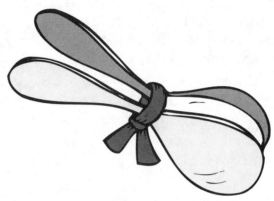

### Coffee Can Drum

Try beating the bottom of a coffee can with a spoon. Try drumming it with your fingers. Which sound do you like best? Glue construction paper to the side of the can to decorate your drum. Trim with washable markers, rickrack or stickers.

### Pie Tin Tambourine

To make a pie tin tambourine, you need one of the thin, foil pie tins. Use a pencil to punch holes around the edges of the pan. Attach a jingle bell, paper clip or any other small metal object to each hole with yarn.

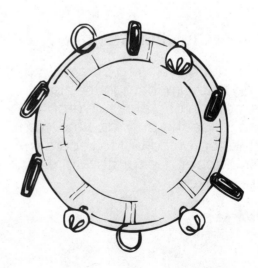

# Old Mother Hubbard's Cupboard Band

### Tissue Box Strummer

**U**se different sized rubber bands stretched around an empty tissue box to make a great sound. Stretch the rubber bands around the box and space them evenly over the hole in the top of the tissue box.

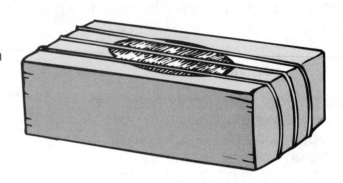

### Tissue Roll Rattle

**P**lace aluminum foil on one end of a tissue roll and secure it with tape or a rubber band. Put rice, beans or macaroni in the tissue roll. Close the other end with aluminum foil and secure. Decorate the side of the shaker with paper cutouts, washable markers or stickers.

### Clay Pot Clanger

**T**ie a nut or bolt to a piece of yarn. String the yarn through the hole in the bottom of a clay flowerpot. Then inside the pot, tape the yarn to the top of the pot to secure the bolt clapper. Decorate with washable markers.

TLC10000 Copyright © Teaching & Learning Company, Carthage, IL 62321

# Oh, Those Round Os

**Directions:** Use **O**-shaped cereal or pasta to decorate the uppercase and lowercase **O**s. If you want to decorate the letters with colored cereal or pasta, add a drop of food coloring to the cereal or pasta before gluing them to the letters. When dry, glue on the letters. Let dry. Cut out letters and attach them to the cover of your **O** folder. Feel the roundness of the letters and the roundness of the things you glued to the letters. **O** is round!

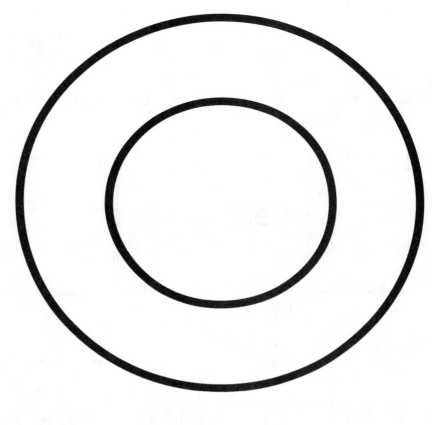

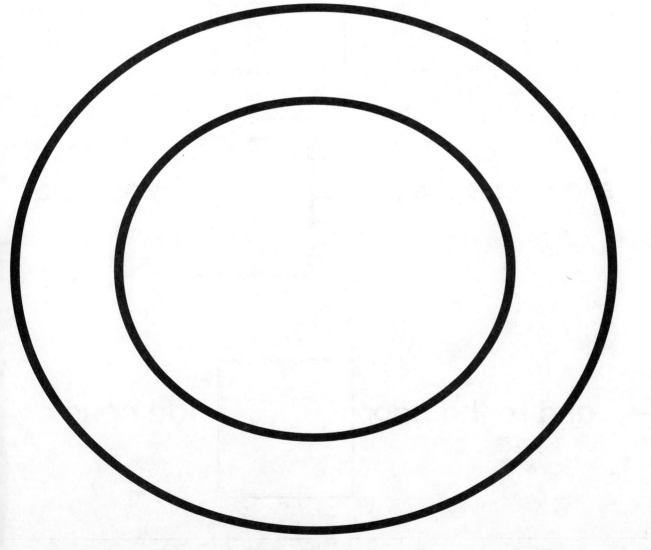

# Rebus Story

To turn the rhyme Old Mother Hubbard into a rebus story, draw an appropriate picture in each box.

 went to the  to get her

poor  a  . But when

she came there the  was bare,

and so the poor 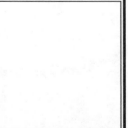 had none.

# Name That O Animal

Cut and paste the name for each animal in the correct box. Then color the animals.

| ostrich | ox | orangutan |
| opossum | otter | owl |

**Game L**

# Old MacDonald's Old-Timer's Band

*Old MacDonald had a farm.*
*E-I-E-I-O*
*And on that farm he had a pig.*
*E-I-E-I-O*
*With an oink, oink, here, and an oink, oink, there.*
*Here an oink. There an oink.*
*Everywhere an oink, oink.*
*Old MacDonald had a farm.*
*E-I-E-I-O*

**Getting Ready:** Practice the familiar song "Old MacDonald Had a Farm" as a group. When everyone knows the words, introduce the animal cards on pages 189 and 190. Color, cut out and laminate the cards. Hold up cards and practice making each animal sound and sing each new verse.

**Directions:** Display the animal cards in the sequence you want them to sing the verses. Practice singing the verses in order. The picture cards will help children remember the order of animal sounds as they repeat each of the previously named animals at the end of every verse.

**Variation:** Use Old Mother Hubbard's Cupboard Band instruments or classroom instruments to accompany the song. Practice. When the class knows the song and can accompany it with instruments, find an audience and perform!

oink oink

cluck cluck

neigh neigh

hee haw

meow meow

honk honk

bowwow

moo moo

baa baa

squeak squeak

ri-bit ri-bit

hissssssssssssssss

# Round O Dishes

*Old Mother Hubbard*
*Went to the cupboard*
*To get her poor dog a bone.*
*But when she came there*
*The cupboard was bare,*
*And so the poor dog had none.*

### Olive Pizzas

Italy

You can make an individual pizza for each student in the classroom. Cover toasted English muffins with pizza sauce, sliced olives and cheese. Bake in 325°F (163°C) oven until the cheese is melted.

### French Fried Onion Rings

United States

1. Let the students peel and cut thick slices of onions with plastic, serrated knives. Carefully pull each onion ring from the slices.
2. Use boxed pancake mix to make batter. Add just enough milk to make a thick, lumpy batter. Dip each of the onion rings into the batter.
3. Have an adult fry rings a few at a time in an electric skillet with plenty of vegetable oil. Use tongs to remove onion rings from the hot oil. Place on paper towels. Serve warm.

### Orange O Rings

Have students wash and peel oranges. On a cutting board, slice the oranges horizontally and arrange on a round platter.

# Outstanding!

_____

knows the shapes of the uppercase and lowercase **O**.

# Outrageous!

You know the sounds the letter **O** makes.

**To:** _____

# Outstanding!

**Y**ou can read these animals that begin with the letter **O**.

- [ ] owl
- [ ] otter
- [ ] opossum

- [ ] ox
- [ ] ostrich
- [ ] orangutan

I'm so proud of the work you have done with the letter *O*.

# Pp

**P**ease porridge hot,
Pease porridge cold,
Pease porridge in the pot nine days old.
Some like it hot,
Some like it cold,
Some like it in the pot nine days old.

**P**at-a-cake, pat-a-cake, baker's man!
Make me a cake as fast as you can:
Pat it, and prick it, and mark it with B,
And there will be enough for Baby and me.

**P**eter Piper picked a peck
Of pickled peppers;
A peck of pickled peppers
Peter Piper picked;
If Peter Piper picked a peck
Of pickled peppers,
Where's the peck of pickled peppers
Peter Piper picked?

# Pease Porridge Clapping Game

*Pease porridge hot,*
*Pease porridge cold,*
*Pease porridge in the pot nine days old.*
*Some like it hot,*
*Some like it cold,*
*Some like it in the pot nine days old.*

**P**resent the rhyme by reading it once to the class. Ask if anyone knows what pease porridge is. Explain that *pease* is an old-fashioned way of spelling *peas*. Porridge is very thick soup. So pease porridge is pea soup. Let the children say the rhyme with you. Repeat as a choral reading. One group says the first and fourth lines. Another group says the second and fifth lines. Everyone says the third and sixth lines. Then play a clapping game. To play, each child will need to sit facing a partner.

| | |
|---|---|
| *Pease porridge hot,* | (Slap knees, clap, clap partner's hands.) |
| *Pease porridge cold,* | (Slap knees, clap, clap partner's hands.) |
| *Pease porridge in the pot* | (Slap knees, clap, clap partner's right hand, clap.) |
| *nine days old.* | (Clap partner's left hand, clap, clap partner's hands.) |
| *Some like it hot,* | (Slap knees, clap, clap partner's hands.) |
| *Some like it cold,* | (Slap knees, clap, clap partner's hands.) |
| *Some like it in the pot* | (Slap knees, clap, clap partner's right hand, clap.) |
| *nine days old.* | (Clap partner's left hand, clap, clap partner's hands.) |

# Peter Piper Puppets

*Peter Piper picked a peck
Of pickled peppers;
A peck of pickled peppers
Peter Piper picked;*

*If Peter Piper picked a peck
Of pickled peppers,
Where's the peck of pickled peppers
Peter Piper picked?*

**T**o practice saying the tongue twisters, talk about the sound of the letter **P** as in *Peter.* Then create and use puppets to say tongue twisters. Directions for making a variety of puppets follow. You may want to set up a learning table with a sample of each kind of puppet and supplies and let students choose which kind of puppet and supplies they want to make. Supplies for making puppets include butcher paper, washable markers, old socks, glue, beads, bits of felt, feathers, red and pink felt pre-cut tongues, peanuts in shells, yarn, lunch sacks, craft sticks, newspapers, tape, string, cotton, straws, toothpicks, plastic spoons, pipe cleaners, cloth, vegetables, fruits, raisins, paper plates and scissors.

## Hand Puppets

1. Make a fist. Be sure that the thumb is tucked under the fingers as shown.

2. Draw two eyes and a nose on the base of the forefinger with a black marker. Use a red marker to draw lips around the gap between your fingers and thumb.

3. Repeat on the other hand. Let your hands have a conversation with each other.

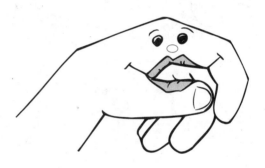

## Sock Puppets

1. If you are right-handed, put the socks on your left hand. If you are left-handed, put the sock on your right hand.

2. Push the sock in between your thumb and the rest of your hand to make a mouth.

3. Use the glue to attach beads, felt cutouts, feathers, etc., to complete puppet's face.

4. Attach a felt tongue. Put glue on the base of the tongue and place it deep inside the puppet's mouth. Let dry.

# Peter Piper Puppets Patterns

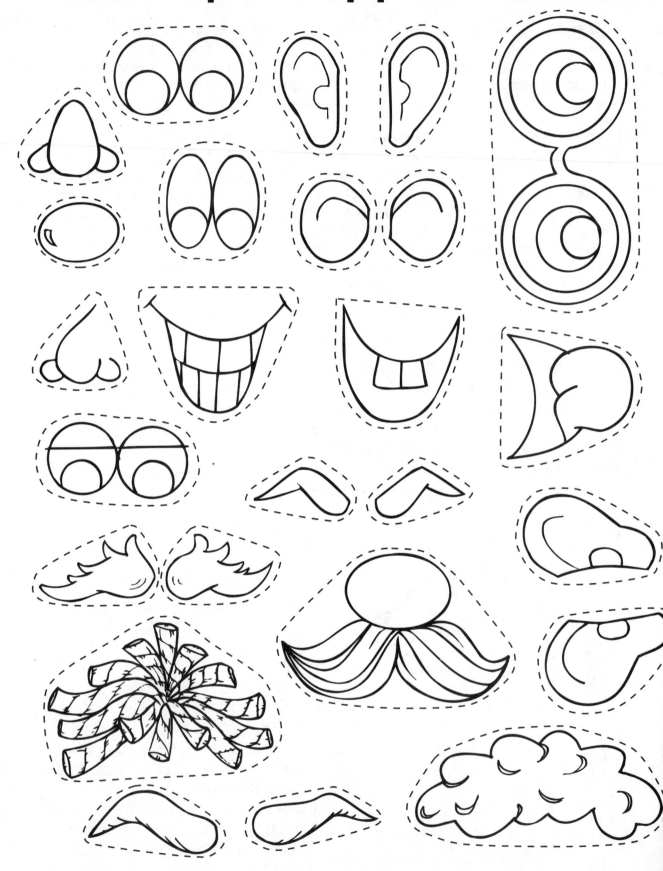

# Peter Piper Puppets

### Paper Bag Puppets

1. Use lunch sacks to make puppets. Draw the mouth where the bottom of the sack meets the side of the sack as illustrated.

2. Trim with paper cutouts, fabric scraps, cotton, buttons, ribbons, yarn and string, seeds or noodles, pipe cleaners, feathers, straws or toothpicks, wire, etc.

### Spoon Puppets

1. Draw a face on a plastic spoon. Glue on yarn hair, whiskers, beard or mustache.

2. Use pipe cleaners for arms.

3. Tie a bow around the base of spoon for a bow tie.

4. Decorate with paper hat or ears.

### Peanut Shell Puppets

(This activity is <u>not</u> recommended for very young children.)

1. Carefully crack open some peanuts. (You may eat the peanuts as you crack the shells.) Use the largest half of the shells for your puppets.

2. Draw a face on each shell. Add bits of yarn for hair, beard, mustaches, etc.

3. Make hats from paper if you like.

4. Decorate the peanut shell puppets any way you wish. Make each one different.

# Peter Piper Puppets

## Paper Bag Puppets

1. Fill the bag with wadded up newspapers and tie with a string.
2. Cut and paste some of the facial features on page 196 to the bag.
3. Decorate with felt cutouts, paper cutouts, yarn for hair, feathers, etc.
4. Place your hand inside the bag.

## Paper Plate Puppets

1. Tape a craft stick to the back of a paper plate.
2. Decorate the front of the plate with paper cutouts, markers, crayons, paints or felt scraps.
3. Glue on hats, ears, whiskers, hair, etc.
4. These puppets can be held in front of the face and used as masks, too.

## Fruit and Vegetable Puppets

(This activity is <u>not</u> recommended for very young children.)

1. Use toothpicks to stick raisins, bits of other vegetables or felt cutouts to vegetables or fruits.
2. You can draw on some foods with water-based markers.
3. Cut a slit in the bottom of the fruit or vegetable and insert a craft stick handle.
4. Glue little strips of cloth around the bottom of the fruit to hide your hand and handle. Vegetables and fruits make really funny-shaped heads.  Try some.

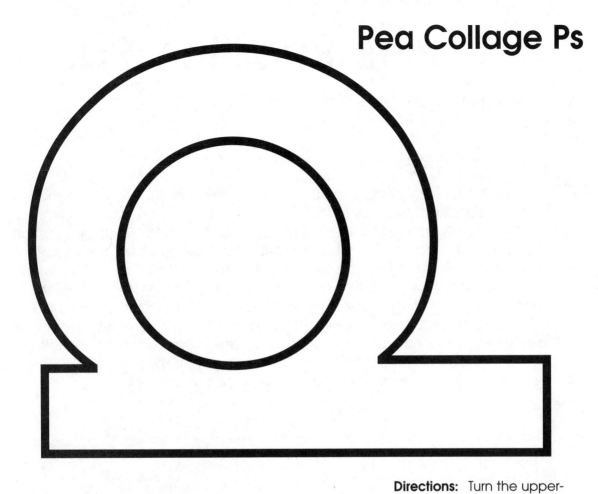

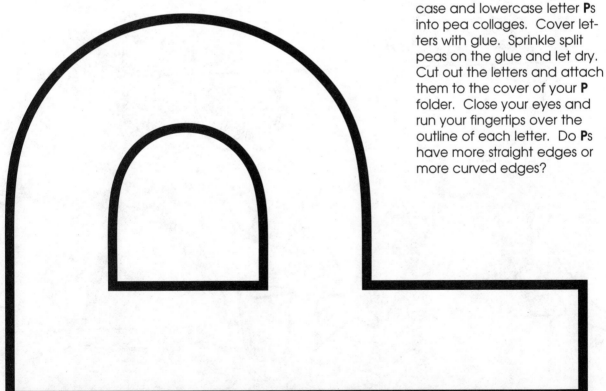

**Directions:** Turn the upper-case and lowercase letter **P**s into pea collages. Cover letters with glue. Sprinkle split peas on the glue and let dry. Cut out the letters and attach them to the cover of your **P** folder. Close your eyes and run your fingertips over the outline of each letter. Do **P**s have more straight edges or more curved edges?

# Pink Pudding Painting

*Pat-a-cake, pat-a-cake, baker's man!*
*Make me a cake as fast as you can:*
*Pat it, and prick it, and mark it with B,*
*And there will be enough for Baby and me.*

**W**riting will be fun when students use pink pudding paint. To make this edible paint, you will need strawberry instant pudding (or color vanilla pudding with red food coloring), milk, mixing bowl and spoon. Mix the instant pudding as directed on the back of the package. Chill until set. Then use the pudding paint the way you would use any other finger paint. It is recommended that you have children cover their work area with newspapers before they begin painting. Give each student a large sheet of finger painting paper and a small paper cup of pudding. Encourage students to use the pudding to print some food words that begin with **P**. Provide a list of words where students can see them as they are writing. Examples: pancake, pie, peanut, pecan, peppermint, pepper, pickle, plum, popcorn, prune, pudding, peanut butter, pear, peach, pastry, pasta.

# Pickled Pepper Pairs

Can you find the peppers that are exactly alike? Color each matching pair of pickled peppers the same color.

# Hot or Cold?

*Pease porridge hot,*
*Pease porridge cold,*
*Pease porridge in the pot nine days old.*
*Some like it hot,*
*Some like it cold,*
*Some like it in the pot nine days old.*

**L**ook at the **P** foods pictured below.  Decide if you like each served hot or cold.  If you like the food best served hot, color it red.  If you like the food best served cold, color it blue.

# Hot or Cold?

*Pease porridge hot,*
*Pease porridge cold,*
*Pease porridge in the pot nine days old.*
*Some like it hot,*
*Some like it cold,*
*Some like it in the pot nine days old.*

**Getting Ready:** Recite the rhyme. Review hot and cold foods.

**Directions:** Play a large group game to reinforce hot and cold. As teacher names objects that begin with **P**, children are to indicate with an action whether the object named is cold or hot. If the thing named is hot, the students fan themselves with their hands. If the object named is cold, they are to wrap their arms around themselves and say, "burr." Explain that sometimes the thing named may be hot or cold, and in this case they can make both actions. For example: Pie can be served hot or cold, so either answer is correct and students can make both actions.

| **Hot** | **Cold** |
|---|---|
| pancakes | pumpkin pie |
| peas | Popsicle™ |
| pumpkin pie | pickles |
| popcorn | peanut butter ice cream |
| potatoes | pineapple parfait |

**Variation:** Recite the rhyme substituting other foods for *pease porridge*.

 P

## Peanut Soup

Sudan/Egypt

1. Grind 1 pound (.45 kg) skinned peanuts (until peanuts are a paste) in a blender or a food processor.
2. Put peanut paste into a large saucepan and gradually add 3³/4 cups (900 ml) milk and 3³/4 cups (900 ml) clear chicken broth. Salt and pepper to taste.
3. Slowly bring it to a boil. Cook for 10 minutes over moderate heat. Stir frequently. Garnish with butter or heavy cream. Makes about 15 1/2-cup servings.

## Peanut Butter Checkerboard Sandwiches

England

You will probably want to make one of these for every 3 or 4 students. With instructions, children can do all of the steps to make these cut sandwiches.

1. Trim crusts from 3 slices wheat bread and 3 slices white bread. Thin sandwich bread works best. Spread 1 tablespoon (15 ml) peanut butter on each slice of bread except one. Stack slices of bread and peanut butter alternating bread colors. Top with the slice of bread without peanut butter. Put the stacked loaf in a plastic sandwich bag and freeze for one hour to firm the peanut butter.
2. Using a serrated, plastic knife, slice the loaf at 1/2" (1.25 cm) intervals to form ribbon sandwiches. Spread the ribboned slices with a layer of peanut butter and on it lay a second slice, turned so that the dark strips rest on top of the white strips. Layer and butter the remaining slices in this fashion. Wrap the loaf and freeze it again for one hour to firm the peanut butter.
3. Unwrap the loaf and slice it to form checkerboard slices.

# P Is for Peanuts

### Peanut Butter Puffs
#### United States

In a medium-sized bowl, mix 3 tablespoons (45 ml) honey, 1 cup (240 ml) crunchy peanut butter, 1 cup (240 ml) chocolate chips and 1/2 cup (120 ml) dry milk powder. Stir until mixture is thoroughly blended. Shape teaspoonfuls of mixture into 1" (2.54 cm) balls. Place finely chopped skinned peanuts on waxed paper. Roll balls in peanuts until coated. Chill and serve.

### Peanut Butter and Jelly Balls
#### United States

1. In a large bowl, combine 1 cup (240 ml) peanut butter and 1 cup (240 ml) dry milk powder. Blend thoroughly. Add 3 tablespoons (45 ml) honey and 2 tablespoons (30 ml) wheat germ to peanut butter mixture. Stir until smooth.
2. Drop from teaspoon 3" (7.62 cm) apart onto buttered baking sheet. Use your fingers to press balls flat.
3. Put 1/2 teaspoon (2.5 ml) of jelly in the middle of each. Fold sides of dough around jelly to seal in jelly. Roll in hands to shape into balls.
4. On a sheet of waxed paper, place 1 cup (240 ml) crispy rice cereal. Roll each ball in cereal until it is coated. Chill.

# Perfect!

_____

knows the shapes of the uppercase and lowercase **P**.

## Proud of You, Partner!

You know the sounds the letter **P** makes.

**To:** _____

## HOT! HOT! HOT!

**Y**ou know what is hot and what is not.

### Pretty Neat!

You made a perfectly crafted puppet!

# Qq

**Q** is the Queen
Who governs the land,
And sits on a throne
Very lofty and grand.

**T**he Queen of Hearts
She made some tarts,
All on a summer's day.
The Knave of Hearts,
He stole the tarts
And took them clean away.

The King of Hearts
Called for the tarts,
And beat the Knave full sore.
The Knave of Hearts
Brought back the tarts,
And vowed he'd steal no more.

# Queen of Q Kingdom

*Q is the Queen*
*Who governs the land,*
*And sits on a throne*
*Very lofty and grand.*

**I**ncrease communication skills with this circle time game. Choose someone to be "Queen" (or "King"). That person sits in a chair at the head of the class. Everyone says the rhyme. Then Queen (or King) asks a question of one student. Example: Can you wiggle your ears? The person answers truthfully. Then Queen asks, "Will you show us?" or "Will you try?" If the person says, "Yes," and demonstrates, she becomes the new Queen. If the person says, "No," the Queen begins with another student and a new question. If a student has trouble thinking of questions to ask, give her one of the following:

Can you whistle?

Can you crow like a rooster?

Can you skip?

Can you hop on one leg?

Can you walk backwards?

Can you sing like an opera star?

Can you count to ten?

Can you name a word that begins with the letter **Q**?

Can you clap five times fast?

Can you turn a somersault?

Can you stand on your head?

Can you run in circles?

Can you touch your toes?

Can you spell your name?

Can you point to something red?

Can you name three people in the room?

Can you write an uppercase **Q** on the chalkboard?

# Q Is for Q-tip™

**H**ere are a few quick craft suggestions using this quintessential tool, the Q-tip™. Quiz your students for some more ideas.

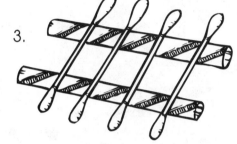

1. Paint with Q-tips™.
   Method A: Use Q-tips™ instead of a brush for watercolors or tempera paints.
   Method B: Wet the paper. Dip Q-tip™ in powdered paint and draw on the wet paper.

2. Use Q-tips™ to make antennae for clay or papier-mâché sculpture.

3. Make railroad tracks out of drinking straws and Q-tips™.

4. Use Q-tips™ to poke holes or scratch lines into wet clay.

5. Use Q-tips™ to apply face paint.

6. Use Q-tips™ dipped in paint to make dot pictures (or freckles, see above).

7. Use Q-tips™ to make a friendly porcupine or cactus out of clay or papier-mâché.

8. Dip ends in glue and use Q-tips™ to make snowflakes. Add string to hang.

9. Use Q-tips™ to make a log cabin.

10. Tie Q-tips™ onto a string and make a "bear-claw" necklace.

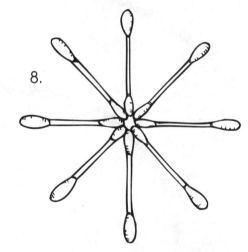

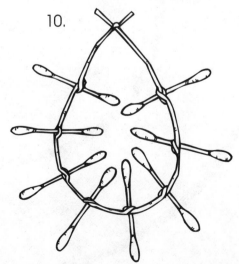

# Quilted Qs

**Directions:** Cut and paste squares of different colors and designs from old magazines. Use them to completely cover the uppercase and lowercase **Q**s. Make the letters look like a quilt by drawing stitch lines with a fine-tip, washable marker around each colorful square. The more colors and patterns you can find to use the better! When dry, cut out the quilted **Q**s and attach them to the cover of your **Q** folder.

210

# Quick as a Wink

Proverbs are short familiar sayings that are commonly used and contain a fact or wise observation. Here are some proverbs for you to discuss with your class. Are children familiar with any of these sayings? Tell what they mean. Can your students come up with some original proverbs?

Quick as a wink.

A stitch in time saves nine.

The early bird catches the worm.

A bird in the hand is worth two in the bush.

You can't teach an old dog new tricks.

# Class Q Quilt

To make a class quilt for the letter **Q**, you need a long sheet of butcher paper, washable markers, colored pencils, pens, crayons, scissors and glue. Print an uppercase and lowercase **Q** on the paper. Then mark off sections so that each member of the class will have his own section. Children can doodle or draw pictures using the uppercase or lowercase **Q** as the basis. Or they can cut out pictures of objects that begin with the letter **Q** from magazines and glue them on the paper quilt. After each student has decorated his section of the quilt, hang it where everyone can see it. A class quilt often makes a good going-away present for a classmate who is moving.

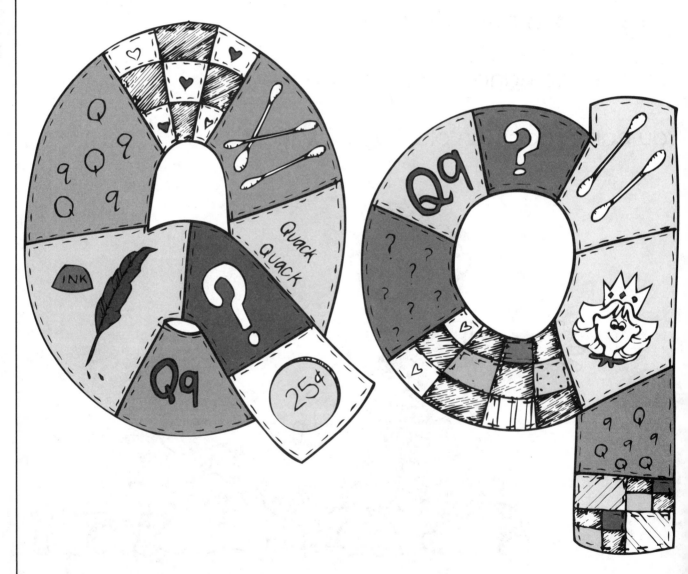

# The Real Queen?

**A**ll of the queens are imposters except one. If you look closely, you will see that each queen has a twin. The queen that doesn't have a twin is the real queen. Can you find her? Color the real queen.

# Q Is for Quiet Times

**Getting Ready:** Talk about what each child likes to do in quiet moments. Discuss how wonderful it is to be calm, quiet and relaxed.

**Directions:** Do some quiet exercises. Examples: I am as quiet as a caterpillar. (Everyone wiggles quietly on the floor like a caterpillar.) I'm gentle as a baby kitten. (Everyone purrs softly.) I am as tender as a teddy bear. (Everyone rocks softly back and forth and hugs himself or each other.) I am as soft as a baby lamb. (Have children feel how soft their hair is.) I am as smooth as a newborn seal. (Have children feel their own skin and appreciate how smooth and pliable it is.) Then have children work in pairs to help each other relax. Encourage deep and slow breathing. Turn off the lights and play soft, quiet music. Stress that this is a quiet time for relaxing.

**Variation:** Have each child stretch out on his back so that his body isn't touching anyone else's. With the lights still off and music playing softly in the background, take the children from their toes to the tip of their head with quiet, relaxing suggestions.

**Examples:** *Your toes are relaxed. They are completely without stress. Your feet are quiet. They feel heavy as if they are made of lead. Your ankles are relaxed.*

Move up the body mentioning each body part and help the children become totally relaxed. After you have quieted their whole body, have them ride an imaginary elevator up, up, up into the clouds where they can float freely for a few minutes. When youngsters are completely relaxed, suggest that they can relax themselves in the same way by beginning with their toes and relaxing each body part. Help them come out of this totally relaxed state slowly and in stages. Turn off the music. Turn on the lights. Let them remain quiet as long as they choose. Others can be dismissed to go outside or to another part of the room so they won't disturb those who choose to remain quiet a bit longer.

# Queen of Hearts Tarts

*The Queen of Hearts
She made some tarts,
All on a summer's day.
The Knave of Hearts,
He stole the tarts
And took them clean away.*

*The King of Hearts,
Called for the tarts,
And beat the Knave full sore.
The Knave of Hearts
Brought back the tarts,
And vowed he'd steal no more.*

## Plum Tarts

Germany

1. Dissolve 1/2 oz. (14.1 g) dried yeast in 8 tablespoons (120 ml) warm milk. Add a pinch of sugar.
2. Put 1 pound (.45 kg) flour into a warm bowl and make a hollow in the center of the flour. Add the yeast. Carefully mix into a pastry. Cover with a cloth and leave in a warm place about 30 minutes until it rises.
3. Soften 1/3 cup (80 ml) butter. Mix butter with 2 tablespoons (30 ml) sugar, a pinch of salt, 1 teaspoon (5 ml) grated lemon rind, 8 tablespoons (120 ml) milk and 1 egg. Add this mixture to the pastry.
4. Knead in the bowl until the dough comes away from the sides of the bowl and is shining smooth. Sprinkle with flour. Cover and let rise again.
5. Preheat oven to 425°F (218°C). Roll out dough very thinly and spread on a flat, greased baking sheet. Sprinkle with sugar.
6. Let students wash and dry 2 pounds (1.9 kg) ripe plums. Slit each plum and remove pit. Open each whole plum and lay flat on dough. Sprinkle with sugar again. Let rise once more for 15 minutes. Bake in the oven for 30 minutes.

## Sugar Tarts

Switzerland

1. Place a ready-made pie crust in a glass pan. Beat 4 eggs with 1 tablespoon (15 ml) sugar. Pour into the pastry. Dot with 1/4 cup (60 ml) butter. Bake until the custard has set firm and the pastry is golden.
2. Mix 1/4 cup (60 ml) sugar, 2 tablespoons (30 ml) butter and 1 teaspoon (5 ml) cinnamon. It will resemble crumbly paste. Sprinkle this over the top of the custard and return the tart to the oven to let the topping melt.

# QUITE NICE!

_____

knows the shapes of the

uppercase and lowercase **Q**.

# Congratulations!

You know the sounds the letter **Q** makes.

**To:** _____

This is a _Q_ for Quiet
Award for

_____

because you know how
to be still.

**Quite
nice
work with
the letter
_Q_!**

# Rr

**R**iddle me, riddle me, ree.
A hawk sat upon a tree;
And he says to himself, says he,
"Oh dear! What a fine bird I be!"

**R**ain, rain, go away;
Come again another day;
Little Johnny wants to play.
Rain, rain, go to Spain,
Never show your face again.

**R**ing-a-ring-a-roses,
A pocketful of posies;
Ashes, ashes,
We all fall down.

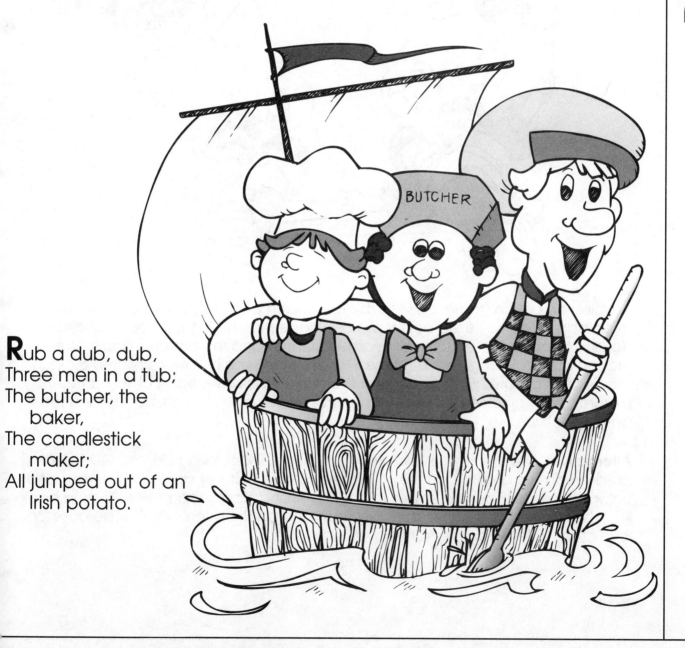

**R**ub a dub, dub,
Three men in a tub;
The butcher, the
    baker,
The candlestick
    maker;
All jumped out of an
    Irish potato.

# Ring-a-Ring-a-Roses

*Ring-a-ring-a-roses,*
*A pocketful of posies;*
*Ashes, ashes,*
*We all fall down.*

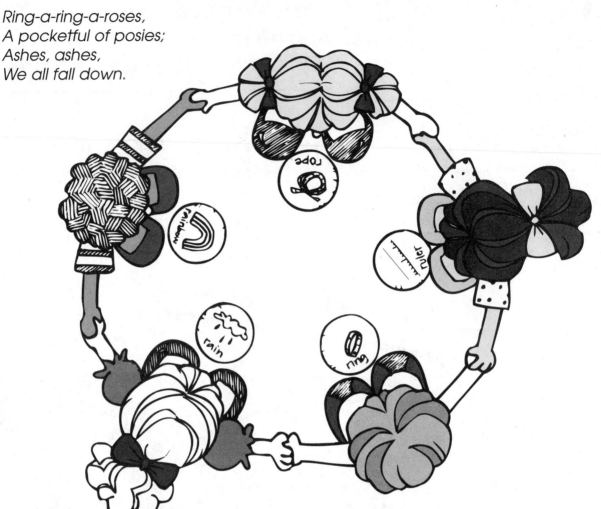

**T**o play an action game with the rhyme, attach each letter **R** picture on the next three pages to small-sized paper plates. Place pictures on the floor in a circle. Holding hands, children form one large circle around the pictures and move around the circle singing the rhyme. When they tumble down, children pick up the nearest picture. Moving around the circle clockwise, each child names his picture. After placing pictures on the floor again, everyone stands up and the game continues.

**Alternative:** Use the letter **R** pictures to make mini **R** coloring books. Give each child a copy of all three pages. Children cut the pictures apart on the lines and color each one. Then assemble in any order and staple together to form a booklet. Use construction paper to make front and back covers. Print uppercase and lowercase letter **R**s on the front cover.

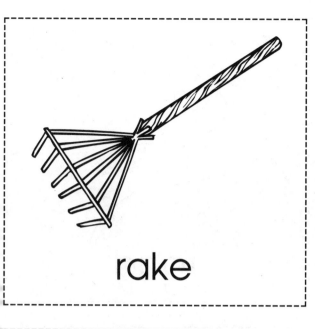

rake

rainbow

rain

rope

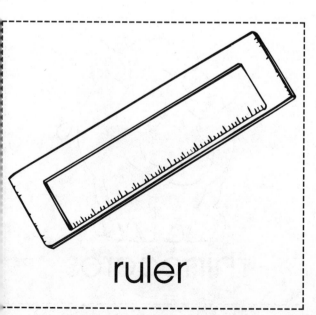

ruler

ring

Ⓡ

**Circle Time**

rock

road

raincoat

rice

reindeer

rhinoceros

robin

raisins

raccoon

rabbit

ribbon

raspberries

Ⓡ

# Rub a Dub Paper Dolls

*Rub a dub, dub,*
*Three men in a tub;*
*The butcher, the baker,*
*The candlestick maker;*
*All jumped out of an Irish potato.*

**U**se the paper dolls and clothes on this page and the next two pages to celebrate the butcher, the baker and the candlestick maker. Reproduce the dolls on heavy paper or light cardboard. Cut out for the children. Reproduce the clothes on white paper. Help the students or let children cut out the clothes. Use crayons or washable markers to color the clothes. Use the paper dolls as puppets to recite the rhyme.

# Rub a Dub Paper Doll Patterns

# Rub a Dub Paper Doll Patterns

# Rhyme Time

Use the letter strips and word cards on this page and the next to create rhyming words. You may want to use these to reinforce beginning letter sounds, spelling words or to create poems! Make your own letter strips and word cards for blends, ending letters, etc.

**Directions:** Cut out letter strips and word cards. Cut the slits on the word cards.

Thread the strips through the slots on the cards. Be sure the letters face front.

Pull the strip to make new words.

b
c
f
h
m
p
r
s
v

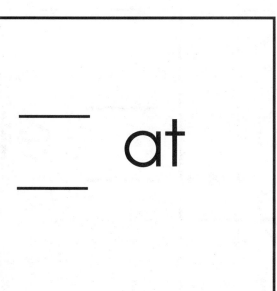

— at
—

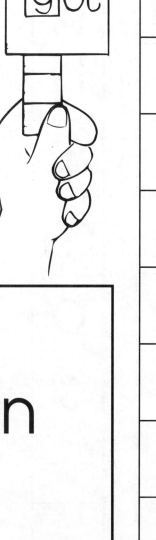

got

b
f
r
s

— un
—

# Rhyme Time

**Others:**
| | |
|---|---|
| **AT** | b, c, f, h, m, p, r, s, v |
| **ET** | b, g, h, j, m, p, s |
| **IG** | b, d, f, p, w |
| **OT** | c, d, g, h, l, p |
| **UN** | b, f, r, s |

| | | |
|---|---|---|
| | b | |
| b | g | c |
| d | h | d |
| f | j | g |
| p | m | h |
| w | p | l |
| | s | p |
| | | |
| | | |

____ ig

____ et

____ ot

**Directions:** To make rainbow **R** collages, you will need 6 paper cups, rice and food coloring. Add food coloring to the cups as follows:

1. 2 drops of red
2. 1 drop of red plus 1 drop of yellow = orange
3. 2 drops of yellow
4. 1 drop of blue plus 1 drop of yellow = green
5. 2 drops of blue
6. 1 drop of blue plus 1 drop of red = purple

Put a tablespoon of rice in each cup. Put glue on each letter and sprinkle on the colored rice. When dry, cut out letters and attach to the cover of your **R** folder. Touch the letters. How does the rice feel? Rough? Rippled?

# Rainbow Rs

# Rosy R Rubbings

...nake rosy **R** rubbings, you will need to provide rose-colored crayons, thin
...er, uppercase and lowercase **R** patterns, scissors and cardboard. Cut **R**
...es from cardboard. Have students put their paper over the surface of **R**s and
...ard with the side of crayon. Encourage them to rub **R**s at different angles on
...oage. Label each rubbing with a black, fine-tip marker: Rosy **R** Rubbing.

...dents enjoy making **R** rubbings, encourage them to gather objects that
...n with the letter **R** to make another rubbing.

**...ples:**
...n

...ck

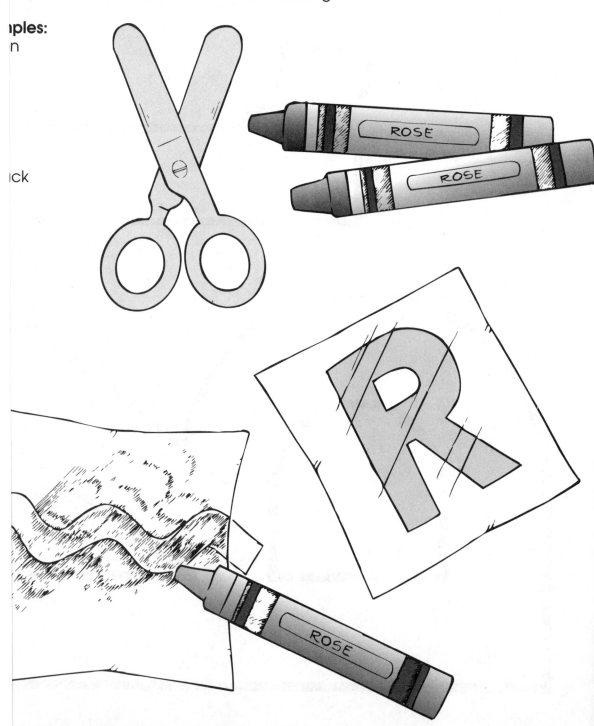

# Raccoon's Garden

**R**accoon is in the garden. *Raccoon* begins with **R**. What other things can you find in the picture that begin with **R**? Look closely and you will see rake, rope, rainbow, rain, rock, road, raspberries, ring, ruler and ribbon. Draw a ring around the **R** things, and then color the picture.

# Rhyming Riddles

*Riddle me, riddle me, ree,*
*A hawk sat upon a tree;*
*And he says to himself, says he,*
*"Oh dear! What a fine bird I be!"*

**Getting Ready:** Many generations of children have enjoyed rhyming riddles. Cut apart the riddle and picture cards on this page and pages 231-233. You may have children color the picture cards and then laminate them. Place the riddle cards in a stack. Place the picture cards on the chalkboard tray or attach to a bulletin or felt board where everyone can see them.

**Directions:** Read a riddle and have students guess which picture is the answer for the riddle.

There was a girl in our town,
Silk an' satin was her gown,
Silk an' satin, gold an' velvet,
Guess her name–three times I've
    said it.

(Ann)

Ann

Formed long ago, yet made today
Employed while others sleep;
What few would like to give away,
Nor any wish to keep.

(bed)

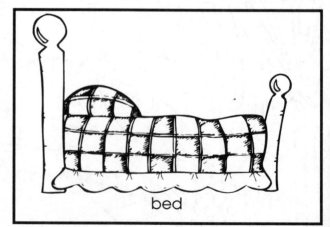

bed

TLC10000 Copyright © Teaching & Learning Company, Carthage, IL 62321

Little Nancy Etticote,
In a white petticoat,
With a red nose;
The longer she stands,
The shorter she grows.


(candle)

candle

Black within, and red without;
Four corners round about.



(chimney)

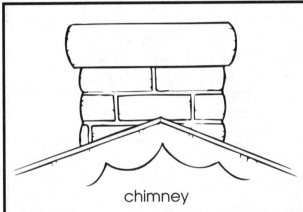

chimney

Humpty Dumpty sat on a wall,
Humpty Dumpty had a great fall;
All the king's horses, and all the
    king' men,
Couldn't put Humpty Dumpty
    together again.

(egg)

egg

I took a walk and chewed some
    gum.
I saw a store selling fingers and
    thumbs!



(gloves)

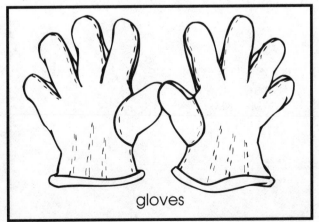

gloves

**R**

**Rr**

**Game**

Riddle me, riddle, me, what is that
Over the head and under the hat?


(hair)

hair

As I was going to St. Ives,
I met a man with seven wives,
Every wife had seven sacks,
Every sack had seven cats,
Every cat had seven kits:
Kits, cats, sacks and wives,
How many were there going to St.
    Ives?

(one)

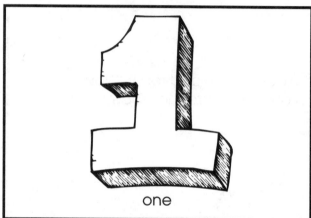
one

Purple, yellow, red and green
The King cannot reach it, nor the
    Queen;
Nor can old Noll, whose power's so
    great:
Tell me this riddle while I count to
    eight.

(rainbow)

rainbow

Higher than a house, higher than a
    tree,
Oh, whatever can it be?


(star)

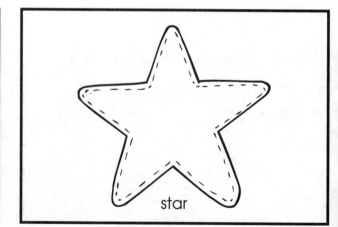
star

R

232

Thirty white horses
Upon a red hill,
Now they tramp, now they champ,
Now they stand still.

(teeth and gums)

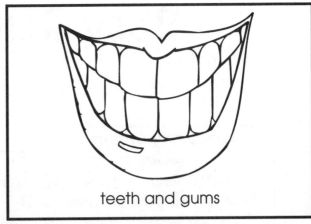

teeth and gums

There was a little green house,
And in the little green house
There was a little brown house,
And in the little brown house
There was a little yellow house,
And in the little yellow house
There was a little white house,
And in the little white house
There was a little heart.
(walnut)

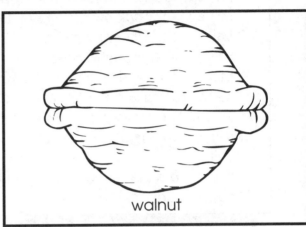

walnut

**R**

# Rosy Raspberry Dishes

### Raspberry Cream
Sweden

To make this dessert, you will need two 12-ounce (340.2 g) bags of frozen raspberries.

1. Put raspberries in a saucepan and add 4 tablespoons (60 ml) sugar. Cook over low heat until sugar dissolves. Add 1 tablespoon (15 ml) butter and 1 cup (240 ml) heavy cream. Stir until thoroughly mixed.
2. Meanwhile mix 4 tablespoons (60 ml) flour with enough cold water to make a paste. When the raspberry sauce is still very hot, remove pan from stove and stir in the flour paste. Return to the stove and stirring constantly, bring just to a boil.
3. Pour into a glass dish, cover and cool. Serve with Danish butter cookies.

### Raspberry Thumbprints
Danish

Danish bakers are famous for rich, sweet, buttery cookies filled with jams. To make quick thumbprint cookies, you will need a tube of ready-made sugar cookie dough or a batch of chilled homemade sugar cookie dough.

1. Give each student a small handful of dough. Shape it into a ball and place it on an aluminum-lined baking sheet. Use a pencil to put the student's initials on the aluminum foil near each cookie.
2. Press the cookie flat with the palm of the hand and then make a deep thumbprint in the center of the cookie. Bake as directed on package.
3. Cool. Fill the thumbprint indentations with raspberry jam.

# Rosy Raspberry Dishes

### Raspberry Sauce
United States

Many children have never eaten raspberries. Even if they are not grown in your area, you can buy bags of frozen raspberries year round. Place frozen berries in a saucepan. Add 1 tablespoon (15 ml) water. Cook slowly. Add 1 cup (240 ml) sugar. Continue cooking until sugar dissolves. Serve warm over vanilla ice cream.

# Remarkable!

_____

knows the shapes of the uppercase and lowercase **R**.

# Right!

You know the sounds the letter **R** makes.

**To:** _____

# Radiant!

**To:** _____

**B**ecause you can read these **R** words.

- ☐ rake
- ☐ rain
- ☐ ruler
- ☐ robin
- ☐ raccoon
- ☐ ribbon
- ☐ rock
- ☐ raincoat
- ☐ reindeer

- ☐ rainbow
- ☐ rope
- ☐ ring
- ☐ raisins
- ☐ rabbit
- ☐ raspberries
- ☐ road
- ☐ rice
- ☐ rhinoceros

## Royal R Award

To: _____

for remarkable progress with **R**.

# Ss

Sneeze on Monday, sneeze for danger;
Sneeze on Tuesday, kiss a stranger;
Sneeze on Wednesday, receive a letter;
Sneeze on Thursday, something better;
Sneeze on Friday, expect sorrow;
Sneeze on Saturday, joy tomorrow.

Sing a song of sixpence,
A pocketful of rye;
Four-and-twenty blackbirds
Baked in a pie.

When the pie was opened,
The birds began to sing;
Wasn't that a dainty dish
To set before the king?

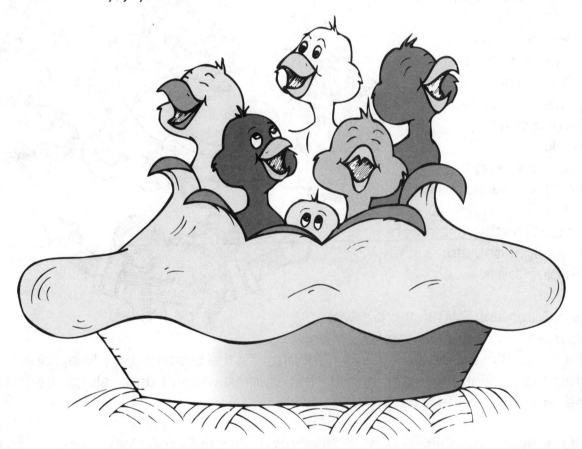

Smiling girls, rosy boys,
Come and buy my little toys;
Monkeys made of gingerbread,
And sugar horses painted red.

Swan, swam over the sea;
Swim, swan, swim.
Swan, swam back again;
Well, swum, swan.

# Sing a Song of Sixpence

*Sing a song of sixpence,
A pocketful of rye;
Four-and-twenty blackbirds
Baked in a pie.*

*When the pie was opened,
The birds began to sing;
Wasn't that a dainty dish
To set before the king?*

**C**hoose several students to be "blackbirds." These children will stand in the center. The rest of the children join hands and form a circle around the blackbirds.
As children sing the first line of the verse, the circle moves to the right. On the second line, the circle continues right and closes in on the blackbirds.

As children sing "When the pie was opened, . . ." the circle moves left and opens up. On the next line ("Wasn't that . . ."), the blackbirds try to escape by breaking through the joined hands. The children whose hands release become the blackbirds in the next round.

**Alternative:** Play a sitting game. Students all sing the song. When you get to the word *blackbirds* in the first verse, teacher points to a student who fills in the blank with an **S** word. Example: Four-and-twenty *shovels*, baked in a pie. In the second verse, sing the new **S** word instead of *birds*. Example: When the pie was opened, the *shovels* began to sing. Give everyone who wants a chance to fill in the blanks with an **S** word to create a silly new song.

# Sneeze on Monday

*Sneeze on Monday, sneeze for danger;*
*Sneeze on Tuesday, kiss a stranger;*
*Sneeze on Wednesday, receive a letter;*
*Sneeze on Thursday, something better;*
*Sneeze on Friday, expect sorrow;*
*Sneeze on Saturday, joy tomorrow.*

**P**ractice singing the rhyme to the tune of "Twinkle, Twinkle, Little Star." When children know the rhyme, replace *sneeze* with a pretend sneeze. Next sing the rhyme replacing the sound of a sneeze with each of the following: snap, sniff, snore, snort.

**Alternative:** Make the rhyme an action game. Teacher names an action. The class sings the new rhyme while one student performs the action. Example: Skate on Monday, skate for danger.

skate
sit
stand
swim
strut
swing
surf
stumble
stroll
stoop
sweep
somersault
sway

Ⓢ

239

# Silly Pies

*Sing a song of sixpence,*
*A pocketful of rye;*
*Four-and-twenty blackbirds*
*Baked in a pie.*

**R**ecite the rhyme. Discuss the idea of blackbirds baked in a pie. Ask the children, "What silly things that begin with the letter **S** can be baked in a pie?" On light-brown construction paper, reproduce the pie pattern on page 241 for each student. Have each student draw something that begins with an **S** in her pie. The sillier the better! If students cannot think of an **S** pie, suggest one of the following:

shoe pie
smile pie
snake pie
starfish pie
sunflower pie
sun pie
skunk pie

snail pie
swan pie
star pie
spoon pie
skateboard pie
skeleton pie

slingshot pie
slug pie
snapdragon pie
snow pie
soccer ball pie
spider pie

# Silly Pies Pattern

**A**fter everyone has drawn his **S** pie, let children share them. Make a list of adjectives that describe the flavors of each pie. Snake pie might be slimy. Shoe pie might be slippery. What is an **S** word that would describe snail pie? (slippery) Sunflower pie? (seedy) Starfish pie? (spiny) Etc.

**Pattern Activity**

# Seashore Ss

**Directions:** Use the seashells on page 243 to decorate the uppercase and lowercase **S**s. Or spread glue on the letter shapes and sprinkle with sand to make them feel like the seashore. Or cover with silk to make them soft, small stones to make them solid or silver glitter to make them shiny. When dry, cut out both of the letters and glue them on the cover of your **S** folder.

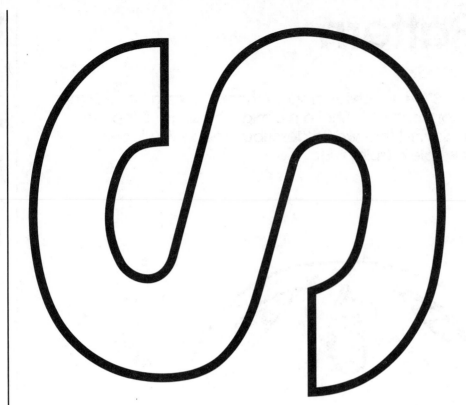

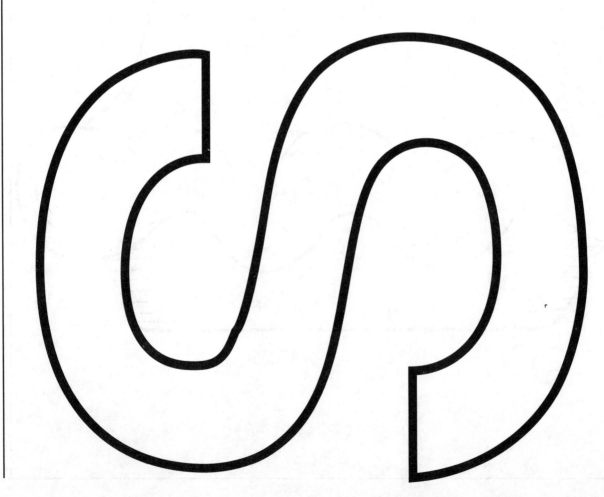

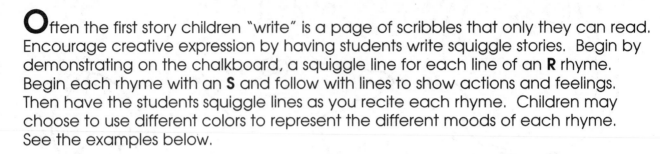

# Squiggle Stories

**O**ften the first story children "write" is a page of scribbles that only they can read. Encourage creative expression by having students write squiggle stories. Begin by demonstrating on the chalkboard, a squiggle line for each line of an **R** rhyme. Begin each rhyme with an **S** and follow with lines to show actions and feelings. Then have the students squiggle lines as you recite each rhyme. Children may choose to use different colors to represent the different moods of each rhyme. See the examples below.

Smiling girls, rosy boys,
Come and buy my little toys;
Monkeys made of gingerbread,
And sugar horses painted red.

Swan, swam over the sea;
Swim, swan, swim.
Swan, swam back again;
Well, swum, swan.

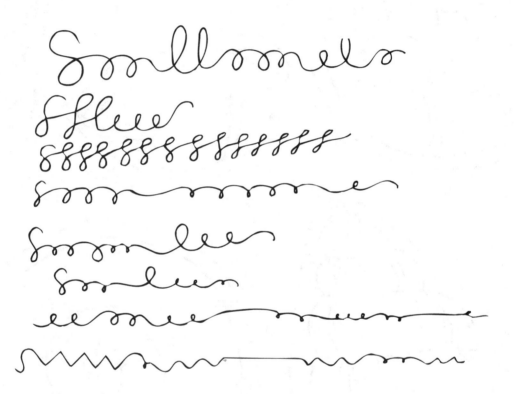

Sing a song of sixpence,
A pocketful of rye;
Four-and-twenty blackbirds
Baked in a pie.

When the pie was opened,
The birds began to sing;
Wasn't that a dainty dish
To set before the king?

Sneeze on Monday, sneeze for danger;
Sneeze on Tuesday, kiss a stranger;
Sneeze on Wednesday, receive a letter;
Sneeze on Thursday, something better;
Sneeze on Friday, expect sorrow;
Sneeze on Saturday, joy tomorrow.

244

# Swim or Soar?

Cut out and color the stamps of animals that begin with the letter **S** on the following page. On the worksheet below, paste each stamp above or below the sea to show whether the animal flies or swims.

**S**

# Puzzle

# Swim or Soar?

# Cut and Paste Ss

**Getting Ready:** Cut apart the word cards below. Cut out and color the stamps of **S** pictures on the next page. Paste each picture on the back of the appropriate card. See game directions on page 248.

| | | |
|---|---|---|
| sun | saw | seal |
| seven | sandwich | sailboat |
| seahorse | sock | sink |
| safe | six | soap |

# Cut and Paste Ss

**Directions:** Look at the word side of a card and try to read it. Turn card over and look at the picture to check your answer. Or look at the picture side and try to spell the word. Flip the card over to check your spelling.

# A Dainty Dish and Strawberry Shortcake

### Strawberry Shortcake
United States

1. Let each child wash 3 to 4 fresh strawberries under cold running water. Remove stems and slice thinly. Sprinkle with sugar.
2. Spoon berries on a shortcake biscuit, slice of pound cake or wedge of angel food cake. Top with whipped cream.
3. Students can whip the cream by shaking it in a jar with a tight-fitting lid for 2 or 3 minutes. Don't shake too long or the results will be butter.

### Chicken Pie
England

1. Cube two cooked chicken breasts. Wash 1/2 cup (120 ml) small mushrooms, 1 carrot and 1 potato. Peel carrot and potato. Thinly slice vegetables.
2. Put the meat, mushrooms, carrot and potato into a pot with 1 cup (240 ml) water. Cook slowly with a lid until vegetables are tender. Drain water and add 1 cup (240 ml) heavy cream in which you have dissolved 2 tablespoons (30 ml) flour. Return to low heat until thick and bubbly.
3. Put a ready-made pastry shell in a glass pie dish. Bake at 450°F (232°C) for 5 minutes. Cool.
4. Pour chicken and vegetable mixture into the partially baked pastry shell. Place another pastry crust on top and seal edges by pressing down with thumb. Bake at 350°F (177°C) for an additional 30 minutes or until crust is brown. When you open this pie, the bird won't sing, but the tasters might!

# Super!

_____

knows the shapes of the uppercase and lowercase **S**.

# Sensational!

You know the sounds the letter **S** makes.

**To:** _____

# Super Reader

**Y**ou can read these words that begin with **S**.

| | | | |
|---|---|---|---|
| ☐ sun | | ☐ star | |
| ☐ swan | | ☐ swan | |
| ☐ shell | | ☐ sea | |
| ☐ sock | | ☐ shoe | |
| ☐ shirt | | ☐ skirt | |
| ☐ snake | | ☐ sheep | |
| ☐ seal | | | |

**I'm so proud of your super effort with the letter _S_!**

# T†

Tweedle-dum and
    Tweedle-dee
Resolved to have a battle,
For Tweedle-dum said
    Tweedle-dee
Had spoiled his nice
    new rattle.
Just then flew by a
    monstrous crow,
As big as a tar-barrel,
Which frightened
    both the heroes so,
They quite forgot their
    quarrel.

Twinkle, twinkle, little star,
How I wonder what you are!
Up above the world so high,
Like a diamond in the sky.

Thirty days has September,
April, June and November;
All the rest have thirty-one–
Except February, alone,
And that has twenty-eight days clear
And twenty-nine in each leap year.

Tom, Tom, the piper's son,
He learned to play when he was
    young.
He with his pipe made such a noise,
That he pleased all the girls and
    boys.

# Sing "Twinkle, Twinkle, Little Star"

**M**ozart wrote the tune for "Twinkle, Twinkle, Little Star" at the age of 6. It is one of the most familiar tunes. It is often used to sing the alphabet song and other songs, too. Hum the tune with the children to make sure they are familiar with it. Most people know the first verse, but very few have ever heard or sung the other verses. You may want to teach one verse at a time since there is a lot to learn.

*Twinkle, twinkle, little star,*
*How I wonder what you are!*
*Up above the world so high,*
*Like a diamond in the sky.*

*When the blazing sun is gone,*
*When the nothing shines upon,*
*Then you show your little light,*
*Twinkle, twinkle, all the night.*

*When the traveler in*
*    the dark*
*Thanks you for your*
*    tiny spark:*
*How could he see*
*    where to go*
*If you did not twinkle*
*    so?*

*In the dark blue sky you keep,*
*Often through my curtains peep,*
*For you never shut your eye,*
*Till the sun is in the sky.*

*As your bright and tiny spark*
*Lights the traveler in the dark,*
*Though I know not what you are,*
*Twinkle, twinkle, little star.*

# Torn Tan T Tapestries

The uppercase letter **T** can be torn from squares of paper by removing two corners as illustrated. Begin this project by tearing squares of tan construction paper for the students. Students are to tear uppercase **T**s from the squares, and paste the letters in an arrangement on a large square sheet of black construction paper. **T**s should overlap slightly and cover at least half of the page.

Use familiar and some not-so-familiar **T** words to discuss the projects.

**Examples:**

tailor
tapestry
tasteful
tasty
tattered
tawny
tedious
terrific
texture
tidy
together
torn
treasure
treat
tremendous

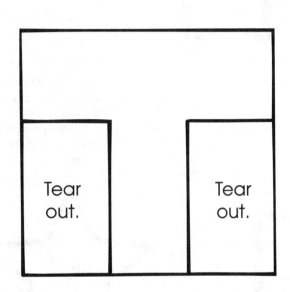

Tear out.    Tear out.

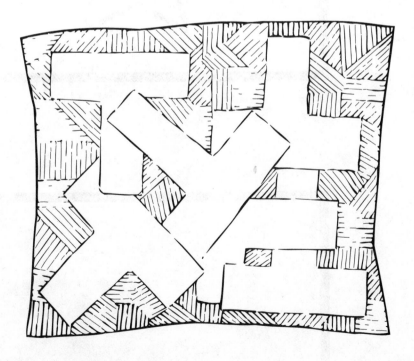

**Pattern Activity**

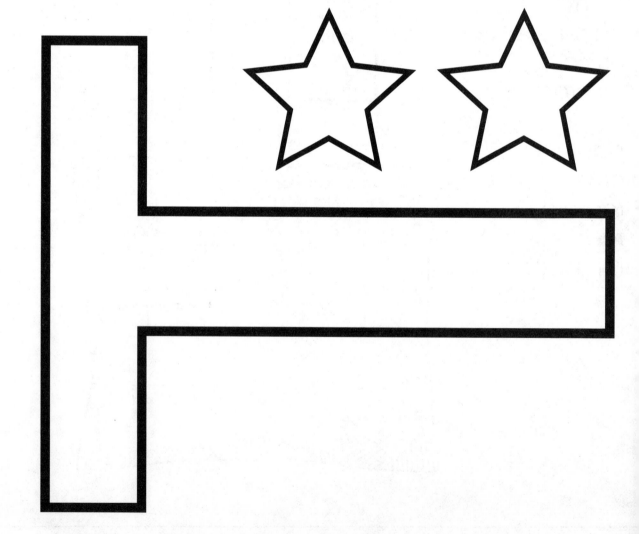

**Directions:** Make the uppercase and lowercase **Ts** twinkle like stars. You can cut and paste the star shapes on each letter. Glue glitter on each one or stick gummed stars all over them. Take your time and do your very best work. When your twinkling **Ts** are dry, cut them out and attach them to your **T** folder.

# Tom, Tom, the Piper's Son

**U**se the verses of "Tom, Tom, the Piper's Son" to have students make a four-page book. Cut out the pages below and the pages on page 256. Students should illustrate each verse and color the pictures.

Tom, Tom, the piper's son,
He learned to play when he was young;
But all the tune that he could play,
Was "Over the hills and far away."

**1**

Now, Tom with his pipe made such a noise,
That he pleased both the girls and the boys.
And they all stopped to hear him play,
"Over the hills and far away."

**2**

# Tom, Tom, the Piper's Son

**S**tudents may want to make and decorate construction paper covers for their books.  Help them print the title of the rhyme on the cover of their books.  Staple down the left side to assemble book.

Tom with his pipe did play with such skill,
That those who heard him could never stand still;
Whenever they heard him they began to dance.
Even pigs on their hind legs would after him prance.

**3**

He met Old Dame Trot with a basket of eggs,
He used his pipe and she used her legs.
She danced about till the eggs were all broke;
She began to fret, but he laughed at the joke.

**4**

# Tic-Tac-Toe Ts

**D**raw or cut and paste pictures that match the words in three of the spaces to make a straight line down, across or diagonally.

| tiger | toes | television |
|---|---|---|
| toast | turtle | toy |
| table | tent | ten |

T

# Thirty Days Has September

*Thirty days has September,*
*April, June and November;*
*All the rest have thirty-one–*
*Except February, alone,*
*And that has twenty-eight days clear*
*And twenty-nine in each leap year.*

**Getting Ready:** Practice the rhyme with your students. If the last two lines are too difficult for the group you are working with, end the rhyme after the fourth line and change the last words like this:

*Thirty days has September,*
*April, June and November;*
*All the rest have thirty-one–*
*Except February which has twenty-eight.*

**Directions:**  Say the rhyme and each time a number is recited, show that many fingers. Thirty is all ten fingers up, close hands, all ten fingers up, close hands, all ten fingers up. This should be done quickly. Then name some of the months and see if the students can figure out that seven of the months, not mentioned in the rhyme, have thirty-one days: January, March, May, July, August, October, December. Children should not be required to learn to name the months or how many days they have, but if they remember the rhyme, someday it will all fall into place, and they will have Mother Goose to thank.

**Note:**  If this game about the number of days in each month is too advanced for your group, play another game that begins with **T**. Try tiddledywinks, tug-of war, tag or tossing a ball. There are tons of terrific things to try that begin with the letter **T**.

# T Is Tasty Tea

In Japan, and other countries, serving and drinking tea is a very special ceremony. In Japan, tea is served from a low table, and people sit on the floor to drink it. Have a tea ceremony in your classroom. Play soft relaxing music. Explain that tea time is an opportunity to relax. Require everyone to speak in a whisper at the ceremony. (Silence is even better.) Removing shoes is also a tradition that you may wish to observe.

## Green Tea with Rice

Japan

Boil 4 heaping teaspoons (20 ml) of green tea with 2 cups (500 ml) boiling water. Remove from heat and let tea leaves settle to the bottom. Put 1/2 cup (125 ml) cold, cooked rice in individual bowls. Pour 1/2 cup (125 ml) green tea over each bowl of rice. Tea leaves can be reused one more time to make another 2 cups (500 ml) of tea. If desired, garnish with roasted chestnuts or pickled cabbage strips.

## Sun Tea

United States

Place 1 gallon (3.78 l) of cold water in a glass container with lid. Put 12 tea bags in the jar and close lid. Sit in the sun for 6 to 8 hours. Serve over ice. Garnish with a sprig of mint, a lime slice or a wedge of lemon.

## Hot Tea

England

Many children have never experienced the delightful ritual of a steaming hot cup of tea. Select caffeine-free black tea, green tea, oolong or a variety of fruity or mint herb teas. Place 1 tea bag for each cup desired in teapot heated by rinsing with boiling water. Bring cold water to full, rolling boil. Immediately pour over tea bags. Steep tea 5 minutes. Stir briskly and serve at once. Provide sugar, honey, lemon, mint leaves and cream to be added as desired.

# Terrific!

_____

knows the shapes of the
uppercase and lowercase **T**.

# _Twinkling!_

You know the sounds the letter **T** makes.

**To:** _____

# Tremendous!

**Y**ou can read these words
that begin with **T**.

☐ tiger
☐ tree
☐ turtle
☐ table
☐ toad

☐ toes
☐ toast
☐ toy
☐ tent

**I'm so
proud of the
work you
have done
with the
letter _T_.**

# Uu

**U** is a unicorn
Who, as it is said,
Wears an ivory bodkin*
On his forehead.

**U**p by the chimney there is a small man,
Who holds in his hands a stick and a fan;
When the winds rage he strikes a fierce blow,
And thus their direction tells mortals below.

**U**pon my word and honor,
As I went to Bonner
I met a pig,
Without a wig,
Upon my word and honor.

*a thick, blunt needle

# Upon My Word

*Upon my word and honor,*
*As I went to Bonner*
*I met a pig,*
*Without a wig,*
*Upon my word and honor.*

Practice the rhyme until the class knows it by heart. Then talk about the rhyme pattern. The last word in the first, second and fifth lines rhyme. The last word in the third and fourth lines rhyme. The idea of a pig in a wig is fun and interesting. What unique animal rhyme combinations can the class invent to create new jingles? Give the students some examples, and then let them make up some of their own. Say the rhyme with each new rhyming word pair.

*Upon my word and honor,*
*As I went to Bonner*
*I met a* ***cat,***
*Without a* ***hat,***
*Upon my word and honor.*

**Examples:**

cat, hat
frog, log
bird, word
mouse, house
toad, road
ants, pants
bee, knee
fish, dish
antelope, cantaloupe
llama, mama
kangaroo, kazoo

# U Is Uniquely You

 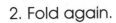
**A**s the students study the letter **U**, explain the definition of *unique*. Then celebrate their uniqueness by making paper dolls. Begin by folding and cutting paper dolls for each student. See the step-by-step directions below and the patterns on the next page. As the children unfold the dolls, explain that each of the dolls is alike, a carbon copy of the next one. People are not like that. Each person is a unique and special human unlike all others. Discuss with the children the things that make each one of them special. Then have the students decorate each doll in a different way.

1. Fold the paper once.

2. Fold again.

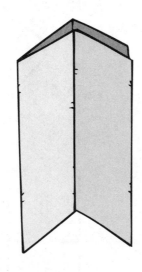

3. Fold one more time.

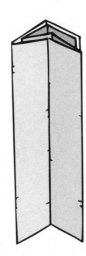

4. Place the pattern on fold and cut out the doll.

5. Unfold.

6. Color and decorate each doll to make it unique.

# U Is Uniquely You Patterns

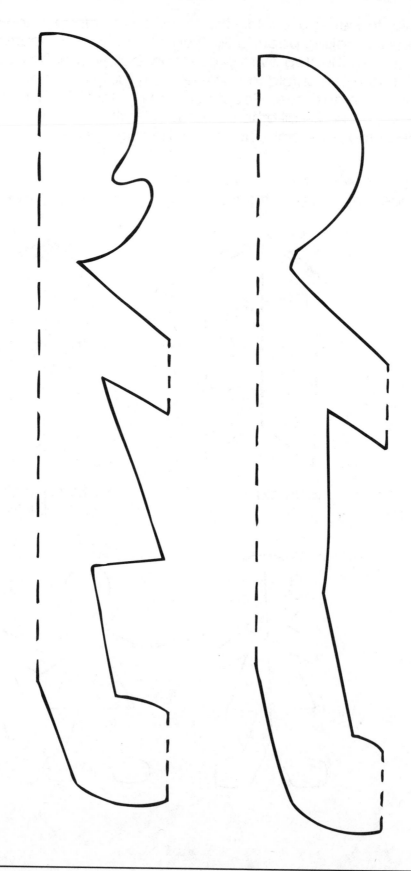

# Unique Us

**Directions:** Decorate the uppercase and lowercase **U**s with pictures and words that tell about you. You may cut and paste pictures from magazines, or you can draw and color your own pictures. Write your first name on the uppercase **U** and your last name on the lowercase **U**. Cut out and attach to the cover of your **U** folder.

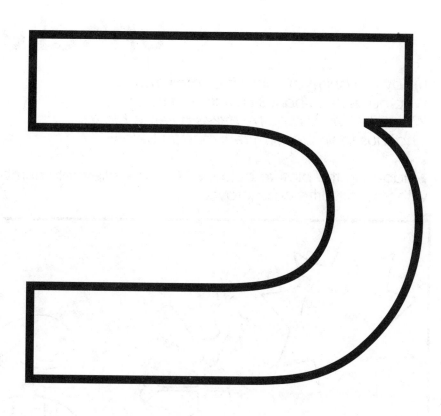

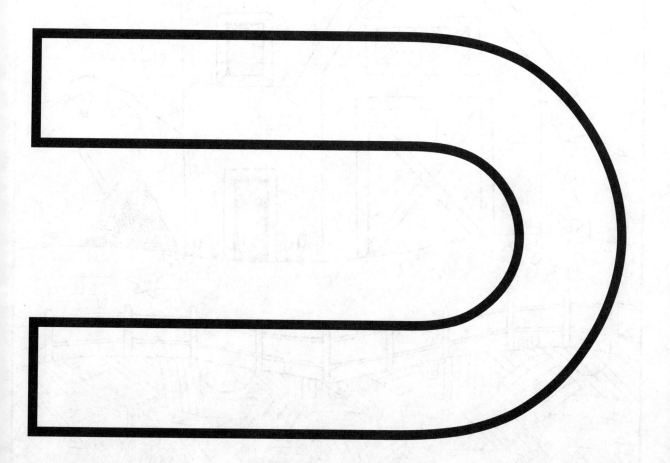

# Unbelievable Us

**Writing Idea**

*Up by the chimney there is a small man,*
*Who holds in his hands a stick and a fan;*
*When the winds rage he strikes a fierce blow,*
*And thus their direction tells mortals below.*

**H**idden in the picture below are an unbelievable number of **U**s. Trace each one with your favorite color crayon.

# Uniquely Me Sandwich

**A**sk someone to help you list your six favorite foods. They may be desserts, vegetables, fruits, meat, anything you like best. What would they taste like all on the same sandwich? Draw a picture of your unique, favorite foods sandwich in the buns below.

Favorite Foods: _____ _____ _____

_____ _____ _____

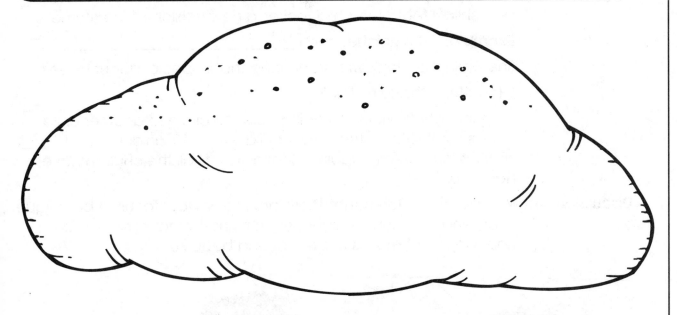

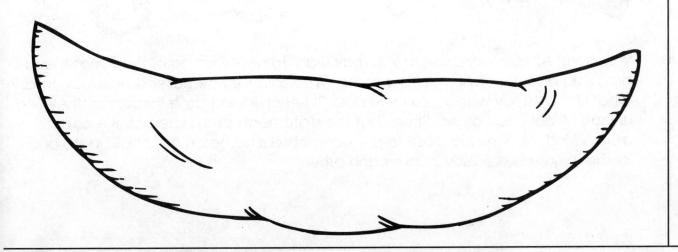

# Uniquely Me

*U is a unicorn*
*Who, as it is said,*
*Wears an ivory bodkin*
*On his forehead.*

**Getting Ready:** One thing that makes a unicorn unique is its horn. What makes each child unique? Ask them to think about things that make them different from others.

**Directions:** Outside, have the class form a big circle. Place a ball in front of one child's feet. The child recites a new version of the rhyme.

**Example:** "**U** is unique, and I _____."

She fills in the blank with something that's special about herself.

**Example:** "I have red hair."

Then she gently kicks the ball across the circle to another child who stops it with his feet. That child says, "**U** is unique, and I _____." and fills in the blank again. Continue until all the chidren have had a turn.

**Discussion:** Remind the children that there are many ways for us to be unique. Every single person is unique, even twins are not exactly alike. Being different makes us special and beautiful.

**Variation:** After the discussion, you may want to review some of the things the children said about themselves. Examples: Who said that he collects baseball cards? What did Rosa say was her favorite color? Let children name things that they find unique about each other. Stress that the statements should be positive and always kind. You may choose to put each child's name on the chalkboard and list the things children say about each other.

# Most Unique Dishes

**W**hat is the most unique dish that each student's family enjoys?  After a class discussion about really special, unique family favorites, send the worksheet below home with each student.  When the children return their recipes, hold a class discussion and share them.  Can the class make and taste some of the dishes?

## Most Unique Family Favorite

Ask someone in your family to list your family's favorite, unusual dish. Talk to that person about the recipe.  Be ready to show the class the recipe and explain how it is prepared.  If you can bring samples, that would be even better!

_____
Title

Ingredients:

_____        _____

_____        _____

_____        _____

_____        _____

_____        _____

Directions:

_____

_____

_____

_____

_____

_____

# UNBELIEVABLE!

_____

knows the shapes of the uppercase and lowercase **U**.

## Unique!

You know the sounds the letter **U** makes.

**To:** _____

## Uniquely You

You can identify some of the things that make you special and different from everyone else!

To: _____

### Excellent!

You created an unusually unique and uniquely you sandwich.

# Vv

**A** is Ann, with milk from the cow.

**B** is Benjamin, taking a bow.

**C** is Charlotte, gathering flowers.

**D** is Dick, one of the mowers.

**E** is Eliza, feeding a hen.

**F** is Frank, mending his pen.

**G** is Georgiana, shooting an arrow.

**H** is Harry, wheeling a barrow.

**I** is Isabella, gathering fruit.

**J** is John, playing the flute.

**K** is Kate, nursing her dolly.

**L** is Lawrence, feeding poor Polly.

**M** is Maria, learning to draw.

**N** is Nicholas, with a jackdaw.

**O** is Octavius, riding a goat.

**P** is Penelope, sailing a boat.

**Q** is Quintus, armed with a lance.

**R** is Rachel, learning to dance.

**S** is Sarah, talking to cook.

**T** is Tommy, reading a book.

**U** is Urban, rolling the green.

**V** is Victoria, reading she's seen.

**W** is Walter, flying a kite.

**X** is Xerxes, a boy of great might.

**Y** is Yolanda, eating bread.

**Z** is Zachariah, going to bed.

# V Is for Vibrations

**E**xplain to the children that vibration is rapid motion back and forth. You can show them vibration by placing a yardstick on a table with a portion of it hanging over the edge. Hold it down firmly on the table with one hand. Pull down and release the free end and watch the stick move up and down (vibrate). Experiment with more or less of the stick extending over the edge of the table. Allow children the opportunity to discover that the more the stick is off the table, the slower the vibration and the lower the sound. The more of the stick that is on the table, the faster the vibration and the higher the sound.

**D**iscuss things that cause vibrations. Examples: When we sit in a car sometimes we can feel it vibrating. When we listen to music played very loudly, sometimes the floor vibrates. Have the children tap a pencil on the table to create a vibration. Have each student place one ear on the table and listen for vibrations.

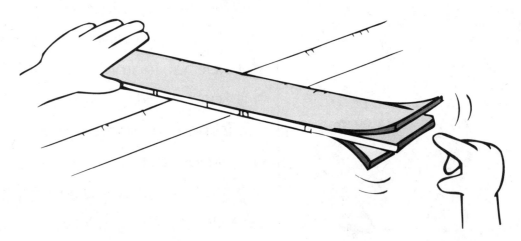

**U**se rubber bands stretched around cardboard, as explained on the next page, or any other method to create a vibrating instrument. Let the children in pairs or small groups arrange a presentation of any rhyme they choose. Then share each arrangement with the class.

# V Is for Vibrations Pattern

**C**ut the **V** shape below from heavy cardboard. Decorate with paints or washable markers. Place different thicknesses and sizes of rubber bands around the cardboard **V** to create a vibrating board. Strum the bands to make different vibrating sounds. Use the vibration board to experiment with rhythm and tone.

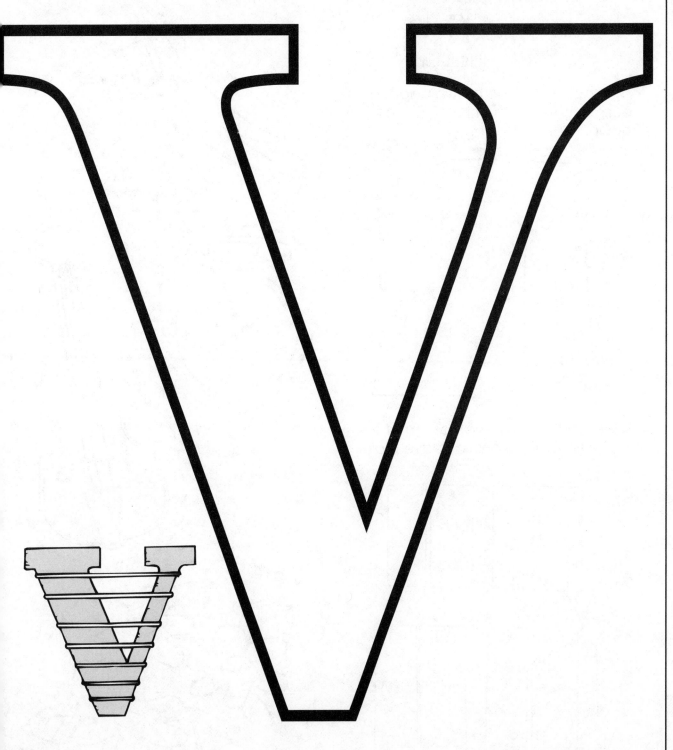

# Best Vest in the West

**D**ecorate with cutouts, sequins, ribbon, rickrack, yarn, washable markers, crayons or other materials.

**Y**ou will need one brown paper grocery bag for each child. Turn upside down. Cut as shown.

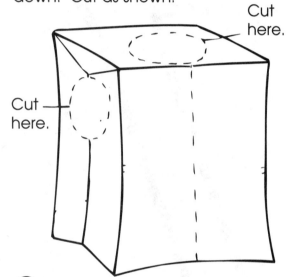

Cut here.

Cut here.

**C**hildren can cut the bottom of the vest (see suggestions) or leave plain.

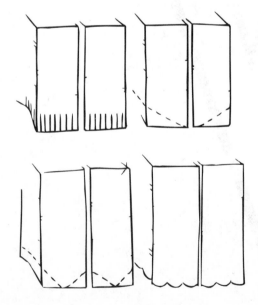

# Velvety Vs

**Directions:** Collect pieces of velvet, corduroy, flannel, chamois and other soft, velvety fabrics. Use the pieces to decorate the upper-case and lowercase **V**s. Make sure the pieces fit inside the letter shapes before you glue them in place. When the glue is dry, cut out the letters and attach them to your **V** folder. Feel the **V**s. Do they feel soft?

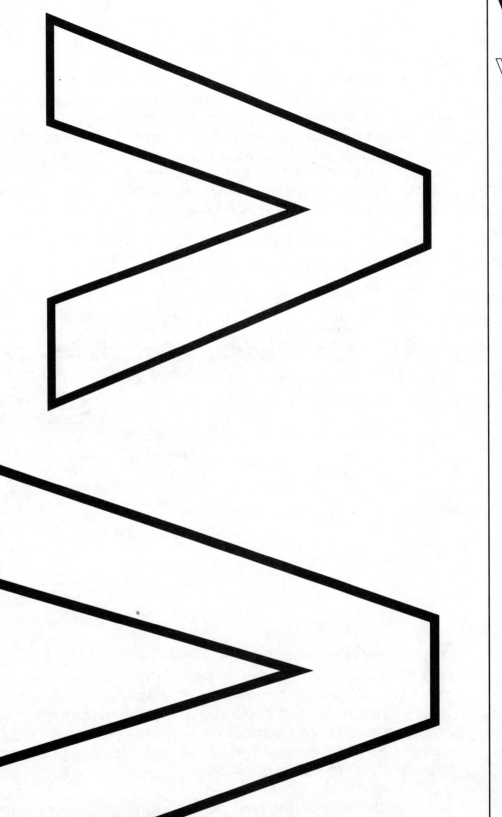

# V Is for Violin

**N**ow that you've made your cardboard vibrating **V**s, it's time to introduce a real vibrating **V**, the violin. Just as your rubber bands moved back and forth across the open space in the cardboard **V**, so do the strings of the violin vibrate over the bridge and resonate between the instument's belly and back. The various tones are produced by lengthening and shortening the string (and the vibration) through the placement of the violinist's fingers on the strings at the fingerboard. The strings are caused to vibrate when a bow is drawn across them or when they are plucked by the violinist's fingers.

**Violin**

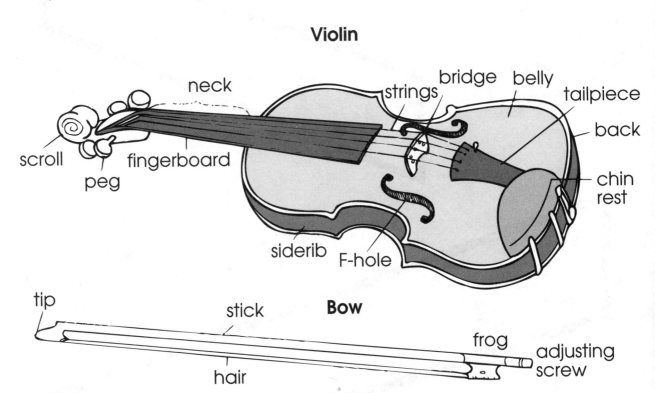

neck · bridge · belly · strings · tailpiece · back · scroll · fingerboard · peg · chin rest · siderib · F-hole

**Bow**

tip · stick · frog · adjusting screw · hair

**Y**our students might enjoy learning more about the violin, viola, violin cello (cello) and other instruments of the orchestra. Your librarian should be able to direct you to reference books and resources. Children may also appreciate hearing how the violin sounds in concert, there are many fine recordings of violin pieces which children can enjoy from vivacious country tunes to Vienna waltzes to virtuoso classical compositions. Of course, one of the best introductions to an orchestra and all its instruments is *Peter and the Wolf*.

**U**se the patterns on the next page to familiarize your students with some of the orchestra's instruments. Ask the children to come up with a list of words or descriptive phrases for each of the instruments.

# V Is for Violin

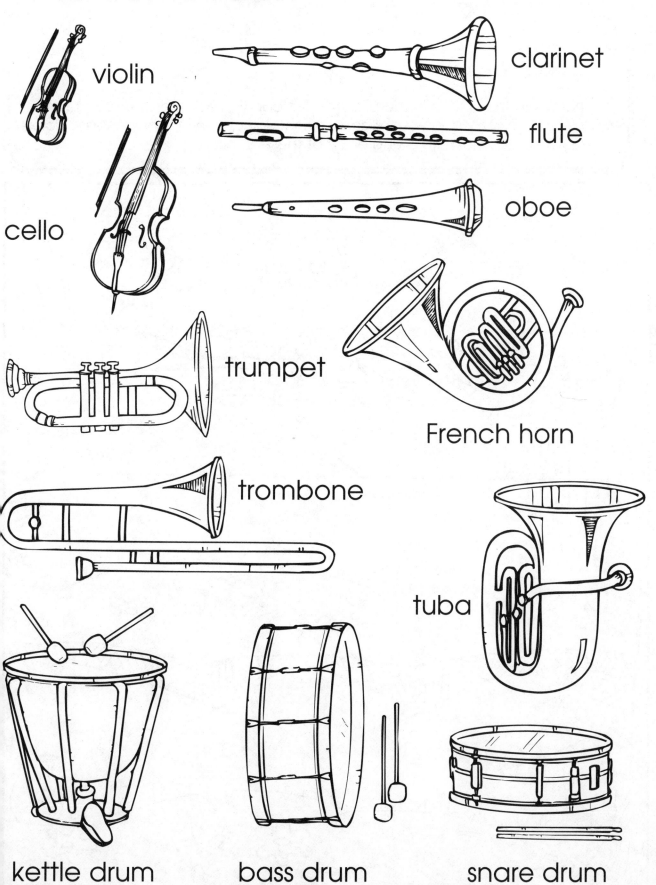

violin

clarinet

flute

cello

oboe

trumpet

French horn

trombone

tuba

kettle drum

bass drum

snare drum

# See the Vs?

*V is a vulture*
*Who eats a great deal.*

**Y**ou can see the vulture in the picture.  But can you see the other hidden **V** things?  Look closely and you will see  a vine, volcano, valley, vest, vase, violets and violin.  Color the vulture and each of these **V** things.

# Very Important Names

**A**fter reading the rhyme, have each child say the first letter of her name and a phrase describing herself. Record these on cards. Then alphabetize them, and read the class rhyme aloud.

**A** is Ann, with milk from the cow.

**B** is Benjamin, taking a bow.

**C** is Charlotte, gathering flowers.

**D** is Dick, one of the mowers.

**E** is Eliza, feeding a hen.

**F** is Frank, mending his pen.

**G** is Georgiana, shooting an arrow.

**H** is Harry, wheeling a barrow.

**I** is Isabella, gathering fruit.

**J** is John, playing the flute.

**K** is Kate, nursing her dolly.

**L** is Lawrence, feeding poor Polly.

**M** is Maria, learning to draw.

**N** is Nicholas, with a jackdaw.

**O** is Octavius, riding a goat.

**P** is Penelope, sailing a boat.

**Q** is Quintus, armed with a lance.

**R** is Rachel, learning to dance.

**S** is Sarah, talking to cook.

**T** is Tommy, reading a book.

**U** is Urban, rolling the green.

**V** is Victoria, reading she's seen.

**W** is Walter, flying a kite.

**X** is Xerxes, a boy of great might.

**Y** is Yolanda, eating bread.

**Z** is Zachariah, going to bed.

**T**o make a class book, use the reproducible worksheet on page 280.

# Very Important Names

Use this reproducible page to make class books. Cut out the page before reproducing. Give each student a copy of this page. He is to copy his own personal card written during the learning game on page 279. Using black, fine-tip markers only, each student is to illustrate his line. Reproduce enough copies of each child's page so that everyone will have a copy of everyone else's page. Alphabetize the pages and turn them into books.

# Everyone's Favorite Vegetable Soup

**V** is for vegetables, one of the most flavorful food groups. **V** is for vitamins, which vegetables give us. Discuss vegetables with your class. Make a list on the chalkboard of all of the vegetables they can name. Then ask each child what her favorite vegetable is. Make a favorite vegetable graph. Ask everyone to bring one of his favorite vegetables to school to make soup.

### Vegetable Soup

Latin America/Caribbean

In Latin America, the range of vegetables is enormous. Meals are most often simple—soups and stews, made with many vegetables and all cooked and served in one pot.

1. To make Everyone's Favorite Vegetable Soup, put 1 pound (.45 kg) of beef with bones and 8 cups (1920 ml) of water in a large pot. Add 3 minced green onions and 2 cans stewed tomatoes. Bring to a rolling boil over medium heat. Reduce until water is simmering and cover. Cook for 30 minutes.
2. While the broth is cooking, help each child, wash, peel and chop his favorite vegetable into chunks or bite-sized pieces.
3. When the broth is ready, strain out meat and bones. Add vegetables and cook for 30 minutes or until vegetables are tender.
4. Serve with bread and butter or crackers.

# Very Good!

_____

knows the shapes of the
uppercase and lowercase **V**.

## _Congratulations!_

You know the sounds the letter **V** makes.

**To:** _____

## _Victorious!_

**I** am proud of the work you completed
with the letter **V**.

## _Very Good_

work with the
letter **V**.

To: _____

# Ww

**W**ash the dishes, wipe the dishes,
Ring the bell for tea;
Three good wishes, three good kisses,
I will give to thee.

**W**ee Willie Winkie
Runs through the town,
Upstairs and downstairs,
In his nightgown;
Rapping at the window,
Crying at the lock,
"Are the children in their beds,
For now it's ten o'clock?"

**W**histle, daughter, whistle; whistle, daughter dear.
I cannot whistle, Mammy, I cannot whistle clear.
Whistle, daughter, whistle; whistle for a pound.
I cannot whistle, Mammy, I cannot make a sound.

# Whistle, Whistle, Whistle

*Whistle, daughter, whistle; whistle,
    daughter dear.
I cannot whistle, Mammy, I cannot
    whistle clear.
Whistle, daughter, whistle; whistle for a
    pound.
I cannot whistle, Mammy, I cannot
    make a sound.*

**S**ome children can whistle. Some cannot. One way to whistle is to make a small **O** shape with the lips. Placing the tongue behind the lower front teeth, and as you tighten the lips, express air out between the lips. Share this method of whistling and let the children practice. Then let others demonstrate how they whistle. Make a list on the board of steps for different ways to whistle. Try whistling in these different ways. Once everyone can whistle in one way or another, divide the group into two parts. One whistles while the other says the rhyme. Then reverse the process, and let the group that whistled say the rhyme as the other group whistles.

**P**lay a whistling guessing game. Let students take turns whistling familiar tunes while the others guess the name of the tune.

**Alternative:** While everyone is sitting in a circle, one student leaves the room While he is out, teacher points to someone who will be the official whistler. When the student returns to the class, everyone pretends to whistle while only the official whistler really whistles. The person who left the room tries to guess who is whistling. When he guesses correctly, he gets to choose someone to leave the room, and the game is repeated.

**Find Out:** What is the longest song that can be whistled without stopping to take in air? Who can whistle on the in-breath as well as the out-breath? Who can whistle the loudest? Softest? Where do we hear whistles? (on the playgrounds, at sporting events, train stations, factories, etc.)

# Weave a Web Dream Catchers

To celebrate the letter **W** as in *web*, weave a web dream catcher. Explain that some Native Americans believe that good and bad dreams float around at night. They make dream catchers out of wooden hoops with a web and feathers that hang down to suspend above their beds. The legend is that bad dreams get tangled in the web and disappear while the good dreams float through the web, down the feather and into the head of the person sleeping under the dream catcher. Discuss dreams and nightmares. Then weave a web dream catcher.

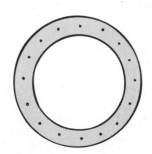

1. Draw a 7" (17.78 cm) ring inside the rim of a 9" (22.86 cm) paper plate.
2. With the help of an adult, cut out the center of the plate leaving the edge as illustrated.
3. Punch 16 holes around the ring.
4. Wrap masking tape around one end of a 36" (.91 m) piece of yarn. Poke the taped end of the yarn into hole 1 and pull it through the hole.
5. Create a web by weaving the yarn back and forth across the plate. String yarn from hole 1 to hole 8, then hole 8 to hole 15, then hole 15 to hole 6, then hole 6 to hole 13, then hole 13 to hole 4, then hole 4 to hole 11, then hole 11 to hole 2, then hole 2 to hole 9, then hole 9 to hole 16, then hole 16 to hole 7, then hole 7 to hole 14, then hole 14 to hole 5, then hole 5 to hole 12, then hole 12 to hole 3, then hole 3 to hole 10 and then hole 10 to hole 1.
6. Attach beads and a feather to each dream catcher as illustrated. Knot the ends of the yarn so it will not unravel.
7. Students can hang their dream catchers over their beds to catch good dreams.

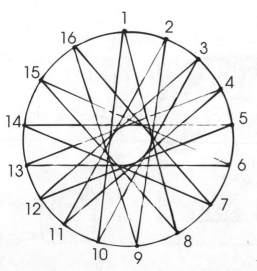

# Wonderful W Washes

*Wash the dishes, wipe the dishes,*
*Ring the bell for tea;*
*Three good wishes, three good kisses,*
*I will give to thee.*

The first step in making wash paintings is to cover the paper with crayon designs. Have the children cover their entire paper with different colors of **W**s. When working with very young, it might be best not to use large sheets of paper. Eight-inch (20.32 cm) squares will probably be large enough. Make sure that they press down heavily with their crayon and that the paper is full of color. Next they should crumple up their paper and dip it in cold water. Squeeze out the water so that the paper isn't dripping. Place on a newspaper and paint over the picture with black paint. Let dry thoroughly before removing from newspapers.

After children become familiar with this painting technique, they may choose to make another wash. Encourage them to choose an object that begins with the letter **W** for their next wash.

**Examples:**

walrus

weasel

whale

woodpecker

woodchuck

walnut

weed

well

wall

# Wonderful Windows

Cut out the bottom row of windows. Glue the top part of the window to the window pictures in the top row. Now lift the flap to see who's inside!

Glue here.

Glue here.

Glue here.

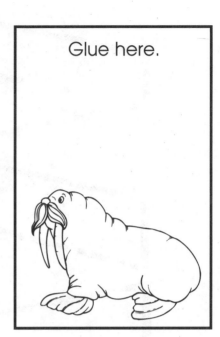

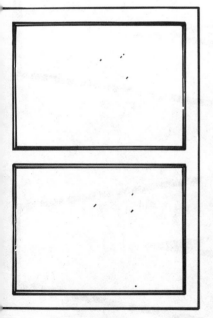

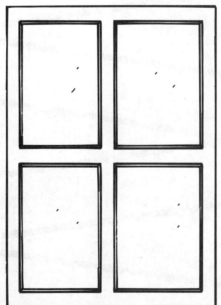

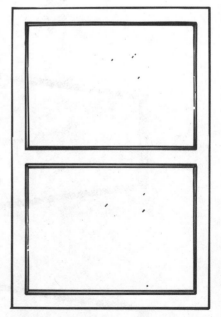

W

**Pattern Activity**

# Wonderful Ws

**Directions:** Illustrate the uppercase and lowercase **W**s with pictures of words that begin with **W**. Worms, wheels, windows, watermelons and watches are just a few ideas. Cut out the letters and attach them to your **W** folder. Are they wonderful?

# Watermelon Wishes

*Three good wishes, three good kisses,
I will give to thee.*

**D**iscuss wishes. Let children share things they would ask for if they could have three wishes come true. Reproduce the watermelon pattern on the next page on red construction paper. Print or have older students record each child's three wishes on his watermelon worksheet. Let each complete his watermelon sheet by coloring the rind green and seeds black. Or attach real watermelon seeds to the worksheets. When everyone has completed his page, assemble into a class book. To reinforce pages, you may choose to laminate or cover each with clear adhesive paper before assembling pages into a book. Read the book to the class. Place the book where members of the class can read it in their spare time.

**O**r use the watermelon worksheets to border a bulletin board or room.

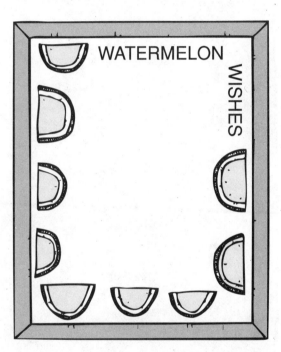

WATERMELON WISHES

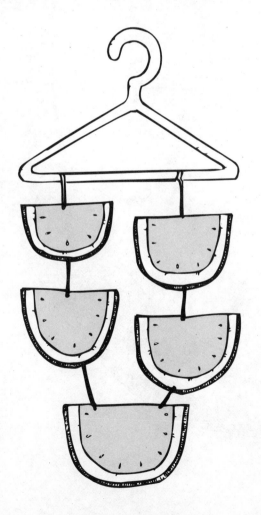

**O**r hang the watermelon slices from a coat hanger to make a class mobile.

Writing Idea

# Watermelon Wishes Pattern

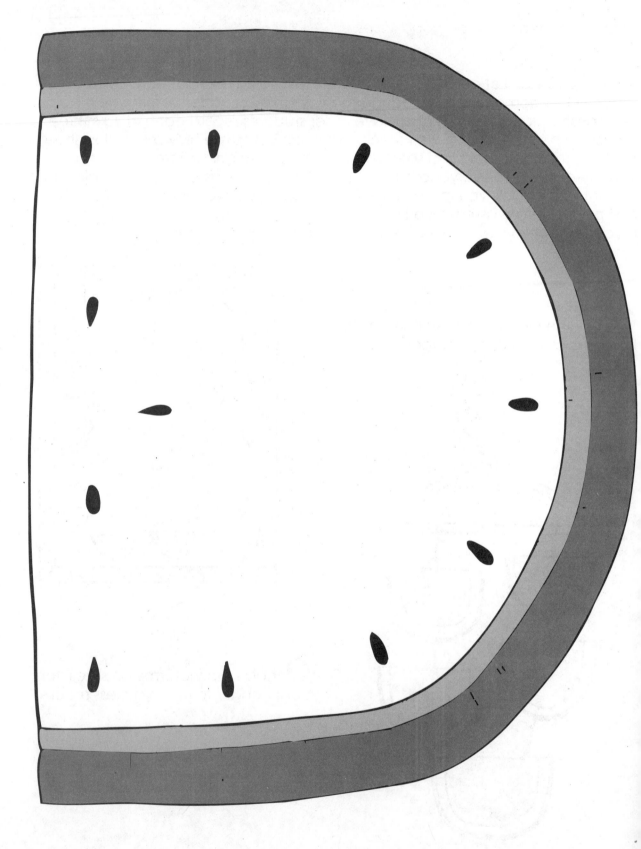

# Wee Willie Winkie

**C**an you see Wee Willie Winkie running through the town? Can you find the other things that begin with **W**? Hidden in the picture are a waffle, watch, worm, wagon, walrus, weasel, whale, woodpecker, walnut and web. Color Wee Willie Winkie and the **W** things you find in the picture.

**Puzzle**

# Wee Willie Winkie

**Game**

*Wee Willie Winkie*
*Runs through the town,*
*Upstairs and downstairs,*
*In his nightgown;*

*Rapping at the window,*
*Crying at the lock,*
*"Are the children in their beds,*
*For now it's ten o'clock?"*

**Getting Ready:** To play this game, children need to have memorized the rhyme. It is best to play this game outside if it is warm and the ground is dry.

**Directions:** Someone is chosen to be Wee Willie Winkie. Then everyone finds a spot that is his "home." Chanting the rhyme, everyone leaves his "home" and runs around. When the last line of the rhyme is said, everyone should scramble back to his original spot and lie down. Anyone caught still wandering after ten o'clock, is chased by Wee Willie Winkie who tries to tag him. If a person is tagged by Wee Willie Winkie, he becomes Wee Willie Winkie in the next round.

**Variations:** After the children have played the game by running, try replacing the word *runs* in the rhyme with *whines, whispers, whistles, walks, waltzes* or *wobbles*. Children chant or move in the appropriate way. Examples: Everyone whines, whispers or whistles the chant, as they walk, waltz or wobble through the town. See if anyone can think of yet another **W** word as an alternative for the chant and game.

# W Waffles and Whipped Cream

## Waffles
### Belgium

1. Sift together 2 1/4 cups (540 ml) flour, 4 teaspoons (20 ml) baking powder, 3/4 teaspoon (3.75 ml) salt and 1 1/2 tablespoons (22 ml) sugar.
2. Mix 2 beaten eggs, 2 1/4 cups (540 ml) milk and 1/2 cup (120 ml) salad oil together until smooth. Add mixture to the dry ingredients. Beat only until moist. Bake in preheated baker. Makes 10 to 12.
3. If you have a lot of students, having several waffle irons in the class will make the baking easier. Or bake the waffles ahead of time at home and reheat them in a toaster in the classroom.
4. Serve warm with whipped cream (see directions below), butter, honey butter (see recipe on page 105), powdered sugar, syrups, jams, jellies or fresh fruit.

## Dessert Waffles
### Germany

1. Beat 2 egg whites until stiff. Blend 2 whole eggs and 1 cup (240 ml) cream together.
2. Stir together 1 1/4 cups (300 ml) sifted cake flour, 1/2 teaspoon (2.5 ml) salt and 1 tablespoon (15 ml) baking powder. Mix with eggs and cream.
3. Melt 1/4 cup (60 ml) butter and add to batter. Carefully fold in the egg whites.
4. Cook in waffle baker. Chocolate chips or pecans can be sprinkled on batter before baking waffles. Sprinkle with confectioners' sugar.

## Whipped Cream
### Denmark

In Denmark, as well as other European countries, food is often prepared with heavy cream.
Children can make whipped cream by shaking it in a jar. Place whipping cream in glass jars with tight-fitting lids, and let the children do the work. Don't shake too long or the whipped cream will turn to butter.

# Wonderful!

_____

knows the shapes of the
uppercase and lowercase **W**.

## Wow!

You know the sounds the letter **W** makes.

**To:** _____

## Whistling Award

**To:** _____

I'm so proud
of the work
you have
done with the
letter _W_.

# Xx

**X** was King Xerxes,
Who, if you don't know,
Reigned over Persia
A great while ago.

**T**here dwelt an old
woman at Exeter;
When visitors came it
sore vexed her,
So for fear they should
eat,
She locked up all her
meat,
The stingy old woman
of Exeter.

**N**ixie, dixie, hickory
bow,
Thirteen Dutchmen in a
row;
Two corporals hold a
piece of twine
To help the Dutchmen
form a line.

# X Marks the Spot

**P**ractice giving and following directions, using graph paper or a grid of your own design.

For younger students, for example:

1. Start at the *X*.

2. Move up 1 square.

3. Move right 2 squares.

4. Move up 1 square.

5. The treasure is on the next square to the left.

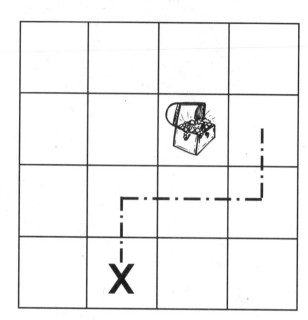

For older students:

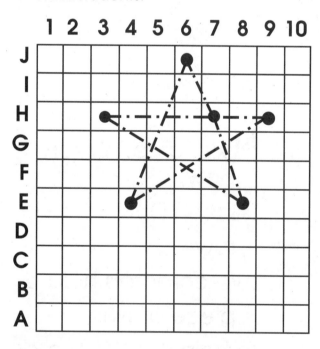

1. Start at E4.

2. Move to J6

3. Move to H7.

4. Move to E8.

5. Move to H3.

6. Move to H9.

7. Move to E4.

8. Did you find the treasure?

**Variation:** Use graph paper to play Battleship.

# Extra-Special King

*X was King Xerxes,*
*Who, if you don't know,*
*Reigned over Persia*
*A great while ago.*

**U**se the pattern below to make an extra-special stand-up king. Color and decorate the king's crown and robe with bright colors and glitter. Cut out and glue around a toilet tissue roll so that the king will stand.

**Pattern Activity**

# Exciting Xs

**Directions:** Cut pipe cleaners as long as the **X**s. Glue them crisscross on the uppercase and lowercase letters. When the glue is dry and the pipe cleaners are securely attached to each letter, cut them out. Attach them to your **X** folder. Close your eyes, and touch each letter. How do they feel?

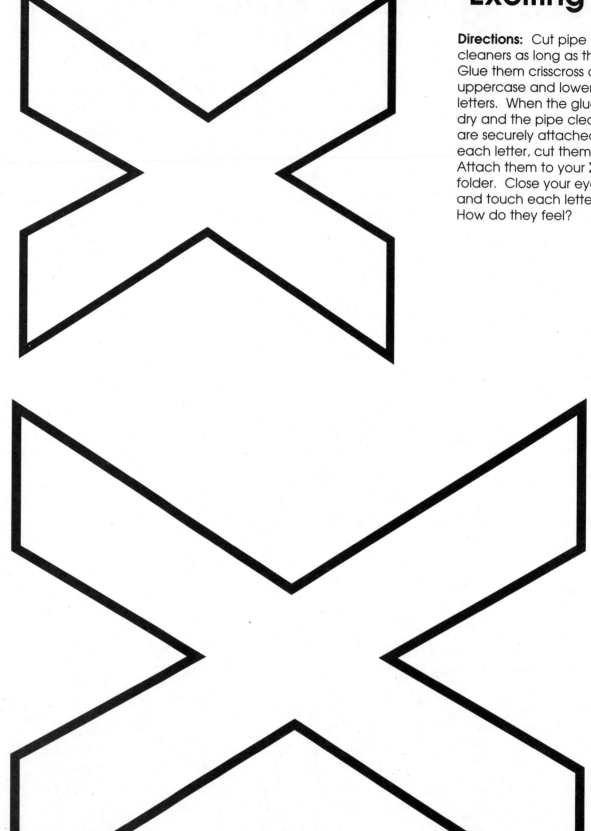

# Extraordinary X Words

Complete each word below by adding an **X**. Then illustrate each word.

fo___

bo___

a___

si___

# Animal X Rays

**D**raw a line connecting each animal with the picture that looks the most like its X ray. Color the animals.

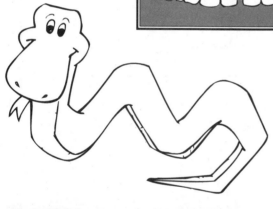
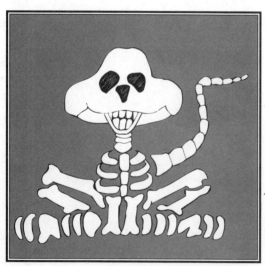

# Nixie, Dixie

*Nixie, dixie, hickory bow,*
*Thirteen Dutchmen in a row;*
*Two corporals hold a piece of twine*
*To help the Dutchmen form a line.*

**T**o discover the mystery shape, color the squares that have a soldier's hat in them.

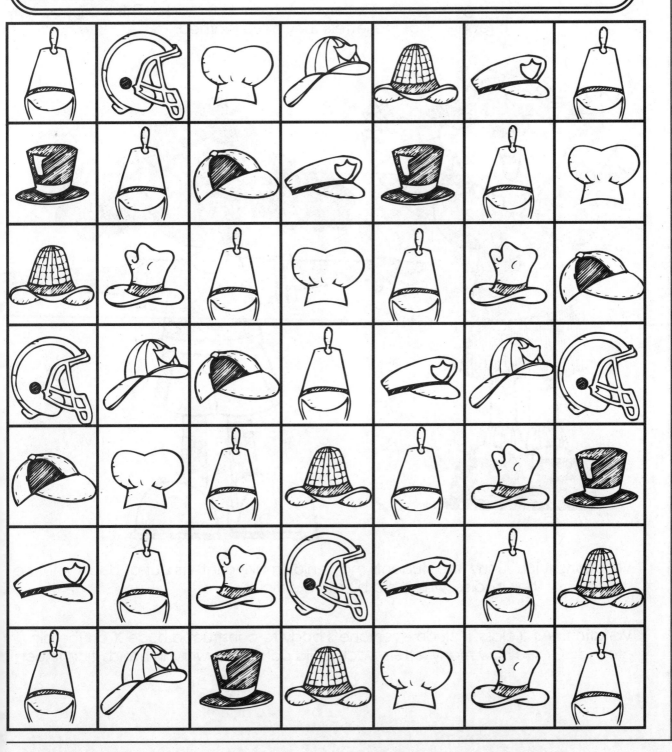

# Body Alphabet

**Getting Ready:** Children can use their bodies to make letters of the alphabet. Have the children work in pairs. Assign each pair a letter of the alphabet. They may choose either the uppercase or lowercase version of the letter. Allow time for each team to practice their letter before sharing it with the class.

**Directions:** As pairs of children use their bodies to make a letter, the rest of the class guesses what letter each team has made. This is a good way to review all of the letters they have learned.

**Variation:** If it is sunny, the students may enjoy making letters out-of-doors with the shadows of their bodies, which is a bit more difficult.

**Variation:** As a class, include everyone's body to construct a huge **X** on the playground. Or see how many letters each child can make with his hands and fingers.

# Extra-Special Burgers

To celebrate the all-American meal, hamburgers, let the children plan a class picnic. To get completely organized, use the questions below and list answers on the chalkboard. Use the list to create a newsletter to be sent home to parents.

Would you like to have a hamburger picnic?
What will we need to make hamburgers?
How will we cook them?
Where will we have the picnic?
How many hamburgers can you eat?
How many buns will we need?
How many hamburger patties will we need?
What condiments do we want?
How much of each thing do we need?
Who can bring each food item? (List names by each item.)
Will we need paper plates, plastic spoons, knives or forks?
Who can bring plates, spoons, knives or forks?
Should we have something to drink?
What shall we drink?
Who can bring paper cups?
Who should we invite?
When shall we have the picnic?

## Barbecued Burgers

Southwestern United States

Celebrate the backyard barbecue tradition by cooking hamburgers outside. For every 6 to 8 students you will need 1 pound (.45 kg) ground beef. Combine 1 pound (.45 kg) ground beef, 2 tablespoons (30 ml) finely chopped onion, 3 tablespoons (45 ml) ketchup, 1 tablespoon (15 ml) prepared horseradish, 1 teaspoon (5 ml) salt and 2 teaspoons (10 ml) prepared mustard. Give each student a handful of hamburger and let him shape it into a 1/2" (1.25 cm) thick patty. Broil over hot coals 5 minutes. Turn and broil 5 more minutes or to desired doneness.

# Extraordinary!

_____

knows the shapes of the
uppercase and lowercase **X**.

# *Excellent!*

You know the sounds the letter **X** makes.

**To:** _____

**Y**ou've done an
exceptional job with the
letter **X**.

## Excellent Work!

# Yy

Yankee Doodle went to town
Upon a little pony;
He stuck a feather in his hat,
And called it Macaroni.

"Yaup, yaup, yaup!"
Said the croaking voice of a Frog:
"A rainy day
In the month of May,
And plenty of room in the bog."

"Yaup, yaup, yaup!"
Said the Frog:  "It is charming
      weather
We'll come and sup,
When the moon is up,
And we'll all of us croak together."

Y is the year
That is passing away,
And still growing shorter
Every day.

**Yy**

**Circle Time**

# Y Is for Yodel

*"Yaup, yaup, yaup!"*
*Said the croaking voice of a Frog:*
*"A rainy day*
*In the month of May,*
*And plenty of room in the bog."*

*"Yaup, yaup, yaup!"*
*Said the Frog: "It is*
*charming weather*
*We'll come and sup,*
*When the moon is up,*
*And we'll all of us croak together."*

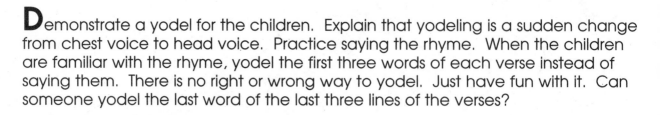

**D**emonstrate a yodel for the children. Explain that yodeling is a sudden change from chest voice to head voice. Practice saying the rhyme. When the children are familiar with the rhyme, yodel the first three words of each verse instead of saying them. There is no right or wrong way to yodel. Just have fun with it. Can someone yodel the last word of the last three lines of the verses?

Yodel "Yankee Doodle," too.

*Yankee Doodle went to town*
*Upon a little pony;*
*He stuck a feather in his hat,*
*And called it Macaroni.*

**Y**

306

# Yankee Doodle Yaks

*Yankee Doodle went to town*
*Upon a little pony;*
*He stuck a feather in his hat,*
*And called it Macaroni.*

**W**hat if Yankee Doodle had ridden a yak to town instead of a pony? After students know the rhyme, have them decorate their own patriotic yak's hat. Reproduce the yak pattern on the following page for each student. Reproduce the hat and feather patterns below on construction paper. Students use the paper cutouts to decorate their Yankee Doodle yak's hat. After everyone has finished, you may choose to play Place a Hat on the Yak game. Simply follow the Pin the Tail on the Donkey rules.

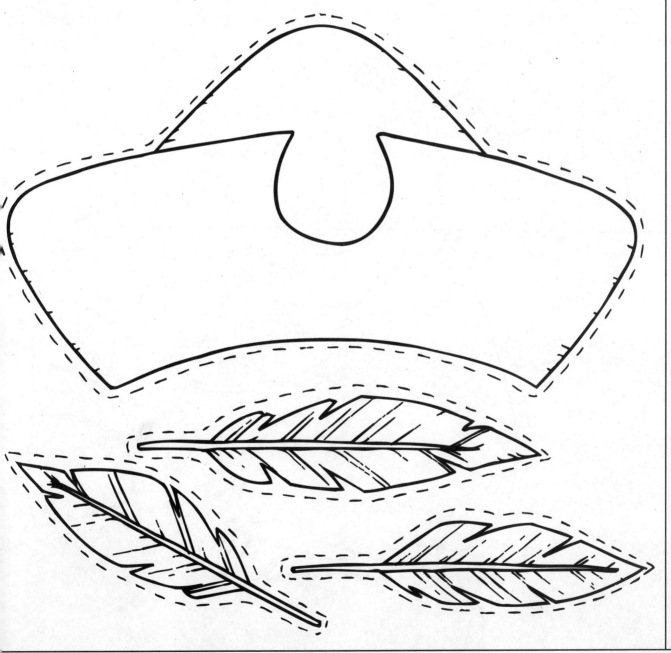

# Yankee Doodle Yaks
# Pattern

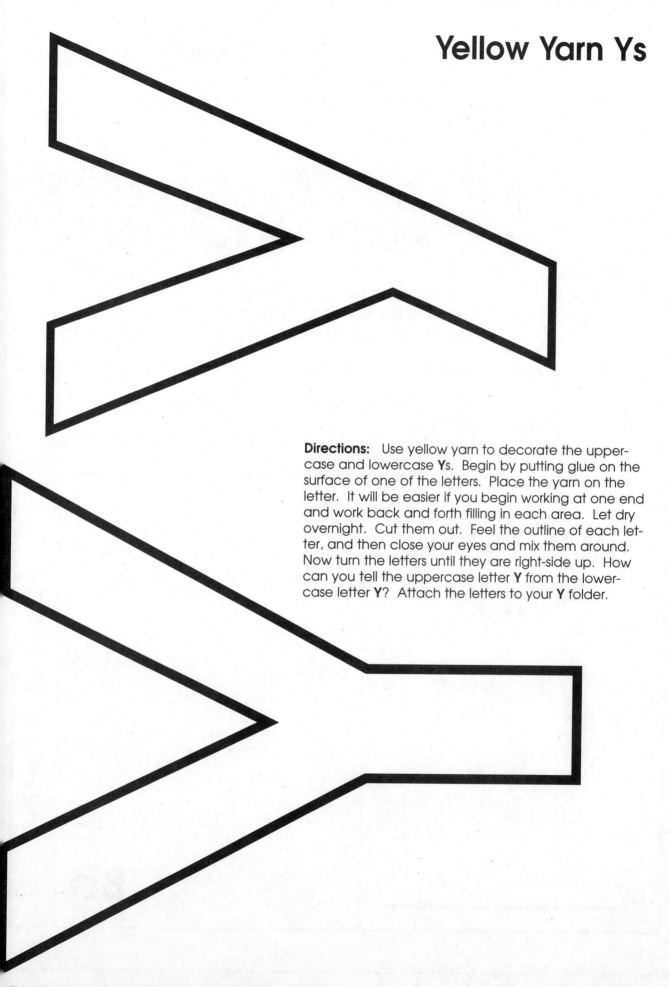

**Yy**

Y

**Pattern Activity**

**Directions:** Use yellow yarn to decorate the upper-case and lowercase **Y**s. Begin by putting glue on the surface of one of the letters. Place the yarn on the letter. It will be easier if you begin working at one end and work back and forth filling in each area. Let dry overnight. Cut them out. Feel the outline of each letter, and then close your eyes and mix them around. Now turn the letters until they are right-side up. How can you tell the uppercase letter **Y** from the lower-case letter **Y**? Attach the letters to your **Y** folder.

**Yy**

## Writing Idea

To make a fold-out ABC book, use the patterns below and on pages 311-313. You may want to have older students help you assemble books ahead of time for younger students.

### Directions:

1. Cut along the solid lines. Line up the pages in ABC order.
2. Overlap and glue along the dotted edges at both ends of each page. Double check to make sure your pages are in ABC order before you glue them together. Let dry.
3. Fold on the dotted line at the center of each page so that the book will fold up.
4. Draw and color a picture for each letter on the appropriate page.
5. Draw a picture on the cover.
6. Print or find someone to print the word for each of the pictures in your book.

# My ABC Book

by_____

## Aa

## Bb

Overlap and glue.

**Y**

**Cc**

**Ee**

**Dd**

**Ff**

**Gg**

**Ii**

**Hh**

**Jj**

**Yy**

**Writing Idea**

**Writing Idea** ◇

| Kk | Mm |
|----|----|
| | |
| Ll | Nn |
| Oo | Qq |
| Pp | Rr |

Overlap and glue.

Overlap and glue.

**Ss**

**Uu**

**Tt**

**Vv**

**Ww**

**Yy**

**Xx**

**Zz**

**Yy**

## Writing Idea

# The Whole Year

**C**ut out the wheel with the seasons of the year below. Glue it on heavy paper, light cardboard or a 7" (17.78 cm) paper plate. Cut out the wheel with the months of the year on the following page. Glue it on heavy paper, light cardboard or a 9" (22.86 cm) paper plate. Trim off the extra paper or cardboard around the edges of both wheels. Put the seasons wheel on top of the months wheel and press a brad through both of them in the center on the **X**. Move the wheels around until the seasons line up with the appropriate months. Winter begins toward the end of December. Color each tree to show the appropriate season.

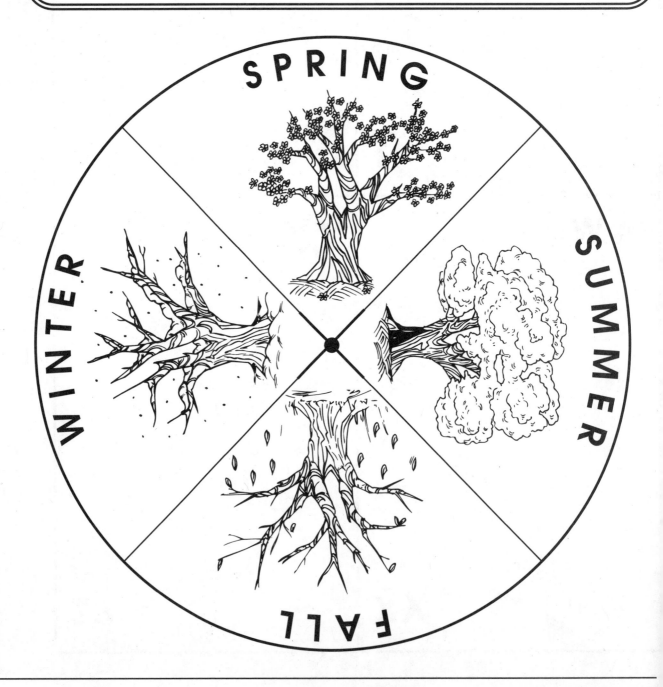

# The Whole Year

Yy

Puzzle

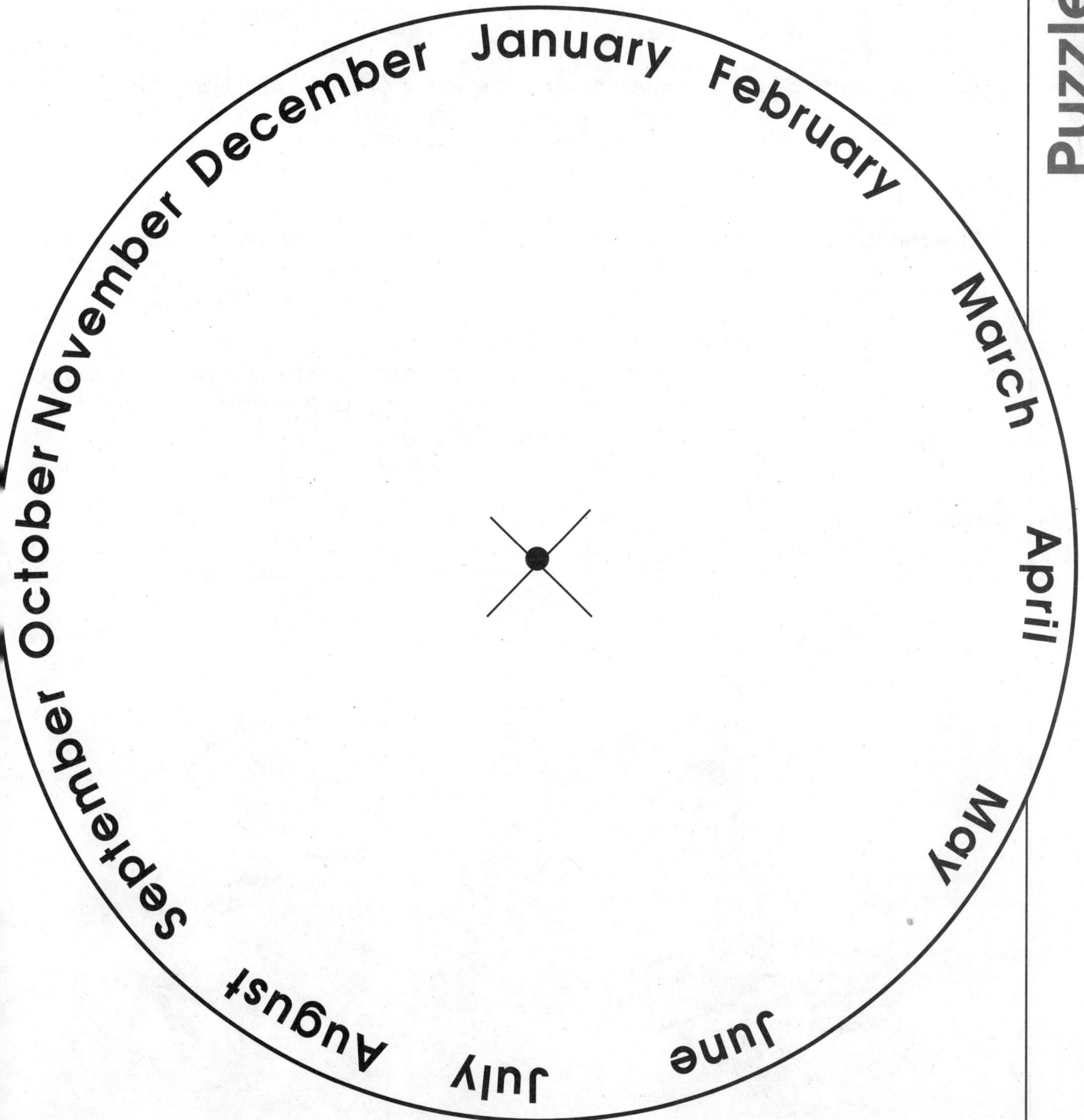
January
February
March
April
May
June
July
August
September
October
November
December

Y

# Yaup, Yaup, Yaup!

*"Yaup, yaup, yaup!"*
*Said the croaking voice of a Frog:*
*"A rainy day*
*In the month of May,*
*And plenty of room in the bog."*

*"Yaup, yaup, yaup!"*
*Said the Frog: "It is charming weather*
*We'll come and sup,*
*When the moon is up,*
*And we'll all of us croak together."*

**Getting Ready:** Say the rhyme. Ask the children if "yaup, yaup, yaup," is the sound they are used to hearing a frog make. What sound does a frog make? Have someone demonstrate the croaking of a frog. Let any who want to croak have the opportunity. Then introduce an animal voices guessing game.

**Directions:**

1. The first player repeats the sound three times he thinks a certain animal makes.

2. Then he points to someone who replies, "Said the voice of the (names animal)."

3. If the person guesses the animal correctly, she gets to give the next clue. If she is incorrect, that player repeats the sound and then points to another student.

4. Game continues until everyone has had the opportunity to make animal voices. Encourage creative animal sounds.

# Y Is for Yogurt–Yum!

*"Yaup, yaup, yaup!"*
*Said the Frog: "It is charming weather*
*We'll come and sup,*
*When the moon is up,*
*And we'll all of us croak together."*

## Yogurt Drink
### The Middle East

Drinking yogurt is popular in the Middle East. It is sold in the streets. To make yogurt drink, mix an equal amount of yogurt with ice cold water. Stir until blended. Season with salt and crushed mint. Serve over ice.

## Yogurt and Cucumber Soup
### Bulgaria

For many centuries, yogurt has been a favorite of nomads and the people of the Balkans. They eat it as a soup at the middle-of-the-day meal. To make yogurt and cucumber soup, you will need 1 pound (.45 kg) cucumbers, 3 cups (720 ml) natural yogurt, 3 cups (720 ml) ice water, ½ cup (120 ml) shelled and chopped walnuts and 2 tablespoons (30 ml) olive oil.

1. Slice the cucumbers thinly. Place in a dish and sprinkle with plenty of salt. Set aside for an hour.
2. Beat the yogurt and water together. Rinse the salt from cucumbers and dry. Add minced walnuts. Pour yogurt and 2 tablespoons (30 ml) olive oil over cucumbers. Pour into bowls and chill.

## Homemade Yogurt
### Bulgaria

1. Yogurt is simply milk thickened by bacteria. To make yogurt, pour 6 cups (1440 ml) milk into a wide, shallow, glass pan. Bring the milk almost to a boil. Simmer gently over lowest possible heat for 20 minutes or until the milk is reduced to 4 cups (960 ml). Remove from heat and let cool to 115°F (46°C).
2. Add 1 teaspoon (5 ml) plain live yogurt. Stir to distribute the live yogurt evenly. Cover with a lid, wrap the pan in a sheet of plastic and thick cloth. Place in a warm spot overnight.
3. The next day, chill the yogurt. Don't shake or disturb the yogurt when putting it in the refrigerator.

# You Who!

_____

knows the shapes of the
uppercase and lowercase **Y**.

# Congratulations, You!

You know the sounds the letter **Y** makes.

**To:** _____

## I am pleased with you,

_____,

because you know the
names of the four seasons.

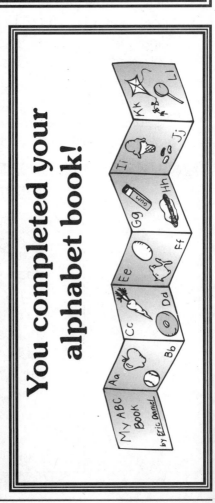

You completed your
alphabet book!

# Zz

**Z** is a zebra,
Whom you've heard of before;
So here ends my rhyme
Till I find you some more.

**A** was an apple pie;
**B** bit it,
**C** cut it,
**D** dealt it,
**E** eyed it,
**F** fought for it,
**G** got it,
**H** had it,
**I** inspected it,

**J** jumped for it,
**K** kept it,
**L** longed for it,
**M** mourned for it,
**N** nodded at it,
**O** opened it,
**P** peeped in it,
**Q** quartered it,

**R** ran for it,
**S** stole it,
**T** took it,
**U** upset it,
**V** viewed it,
**W** wanted it,
**X, Y, Z** and ampersand
All wished for a piece in
    hand.

# Sing a Song A to Z

*A, B, C, D, E, F, G,*
*H, I, J, K, L, M, N, O, P,*
*Q, R, S, T, U, V, W, X, Y, Z.*
*Now I know my ABCs.*
*Aren't you very proud of me?*

**M**ost children have heard "The Alphabet Song" sung to the tune of "Twinkle, Twinkle, Little Star." Practice singing the letters to make sure everyone can say the letters from start to finish. Then play a relay singing game.

**T**eacher points to a student who sings **A**. Then she points to another student who sings **B**. See if the children can keep the rhythm and tune of the song as letters are sung by different children. Teacher directs the alphabet choir with hand signals. This kind of singing in relay can be fun. When everyone knows the tune and alphabet, try speeding up the song a bit. Don't put anyone on the spot. If a student doesn't know the letter, sing it for her so the song will not stop or be interrupted.

**Alternative:** Have the groups sing alternating letters. Example: Boys begin with **A**. Girls chime in with B, etc., or break it into lines as follows:

| | |
|---|---|
| *A, B, C, D, E, F, G,* | Group 1 |
| *H, I, J, K, L, M, N, O, P,* | Group 2 |
| *Q, R, S,* | Group 1 |
| *T, U, V,* | Group 2 |
| *W, X,* | Group 1 |
| *Y, Z.* | Group 2 |
| *Now I know my ABCs.* | All |
| *Aren't you very proud of me?* | |

**Z**

# Alphabet Exchange

**A**ssign each child a letter of the alphabet. (For young children you may want to write the letter on a card or provide a plastic letter shape to help them remember.) Children stand or sit in a circle, except for one child who stands or sits in the center. The child in the center (or the teacher) calls out two letters of the alphabet. The children whose letters are called try to exchange places while the child in the center tries to get to one of the empty places first. The player left standing goes to the center for the next round.

# Hairy, Green Zebra

*A, B, C, D, E, F, G,*
*H, I, J, K, L, M, N, O, P,*
*Q, R, S, T, U, V, W, X, Y, Z.*
*Now I know my ABCs.*
*Aren't you very proud of me?*

**T**o make a hairy, green zebra to celebrate **Z**s, students will need the pattern below, a Styrofoam™ cup, potting soil and grass seed.  Fill each cup nearly full of potting soil.  Sprinkle grass seed on the soil.  Lightly cover seeds with soil.  Use a green crayon to color some of the zebra's stripes.  Cut out the zebra and glue it to the cup.  Place in a sunny spot and water enough to keep the soil moist.  In 10 to 14 days, the green zebras will grow green hair.

# Zebra-Stripped Zs

**Directions:** Decorate the **Z**s by coloring them with zebra stripes. Use only black and white crayons or alternately color stripes with a black, washable marker. When your **Z**s look zebra-like, cut out the letters and glue them to the cover of your **Z** folder.

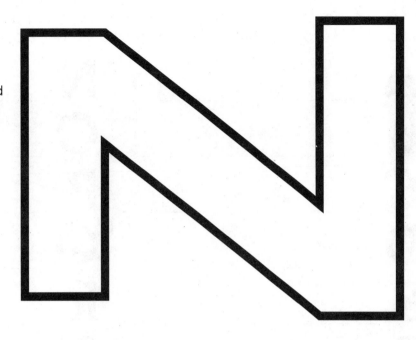

# Alphabet Scavenger Hunt

**H**ave students look in books and magazines to find a word that begins with each letter. Copy each word next to the correct letter below.

A _____

B _____

C _____

D _____

E _____

F _____

G _____

H _____

I _____

J _____

K _____

L _____

M _____

N _____

O _____

P _____

Q _____

R _____

S _____

T _____

U _____

V _____

W _____

X _____

Y _____

Z _____

# Zoo Search

Somewhere in the zoo is an animal for every letter of the alphabet. Can you find alligator, bird, cat, dog, elephant, fish, goat, horse, iguana, jellyfish, kangaroo, llama, monkey, newt, ostrich, porcupine, quail, rhinoceros, snake, turtle, unicorn, vulture, walrus, xenopus (a toad), yak and zebra? Next to each animal, print that animal's initial letter. Color the picture.

# Zoo Animal Matchup

*Z is a zebra,*
*Whom you've heard of before;*
*So here ends my rhyme*
*Till I find you some more.*

**Getting Ready:** Reproduce cards (pages 326-331) on heavy paper or light cardboard. Color and cut apart. For more durability, laminate or cover with clear adhesive paper.

**Directions:** This game can be played by 2 to 4 players. Shuffle cards and deal seven to each player. Place the rest of the cards facedown in the center of players. First player draws a card. He looks to see if he has a matching pair of cards in his hand. If he does, he lays them down in front of him. Then he discards one card from his hand. The next player can draw the card on the top of the deck or take the last card that was discarded. There are two wild cards in the deck, and they can be used with any animal to make a pair. If there are no more cards to select from, the discard pile is shuffled and placed facedown. The game continues until one player has made four pairs and is declared the winner.

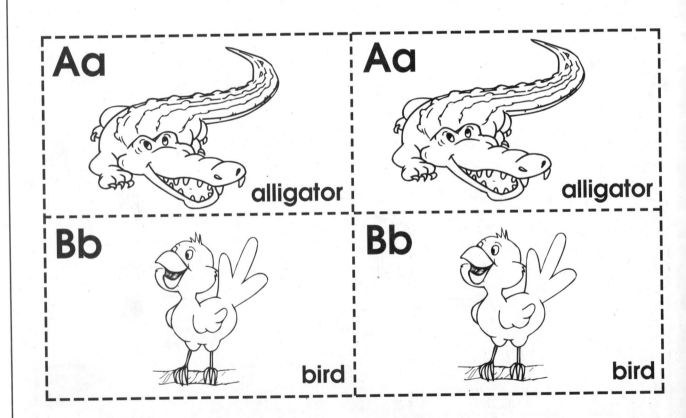

TLC10000 Copyright © Teaching & Learning Company, Carthage, IL 62321

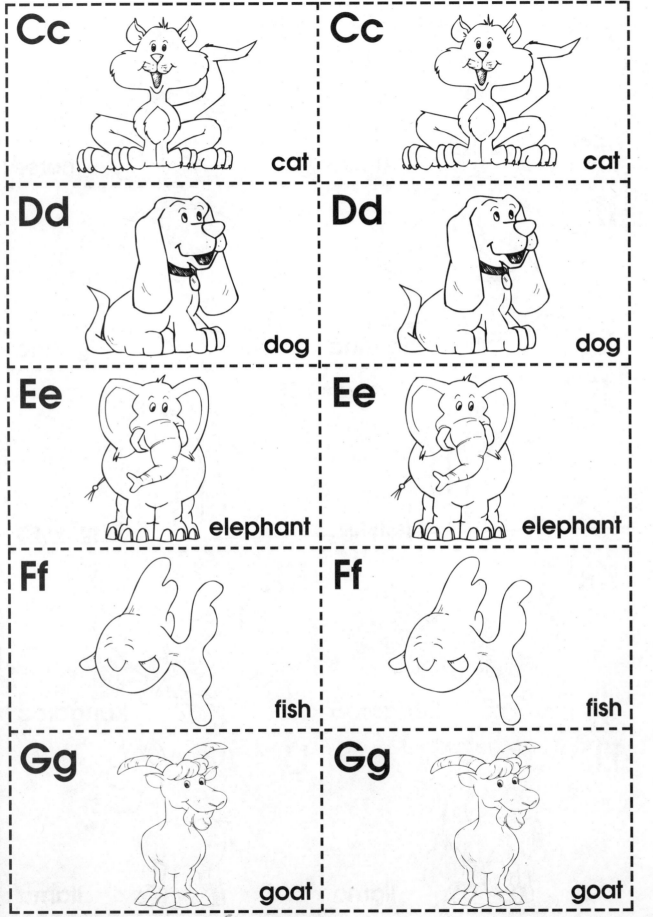

**Cc** cat

**Cc** cat

**Dd** dog

**Dd** dog

**Ee** elephant

**Ee** elephant

**Ff** fish

**Ff** fish

**Gg** goat

**Gg** goat

**Zz**

**Game**

Z

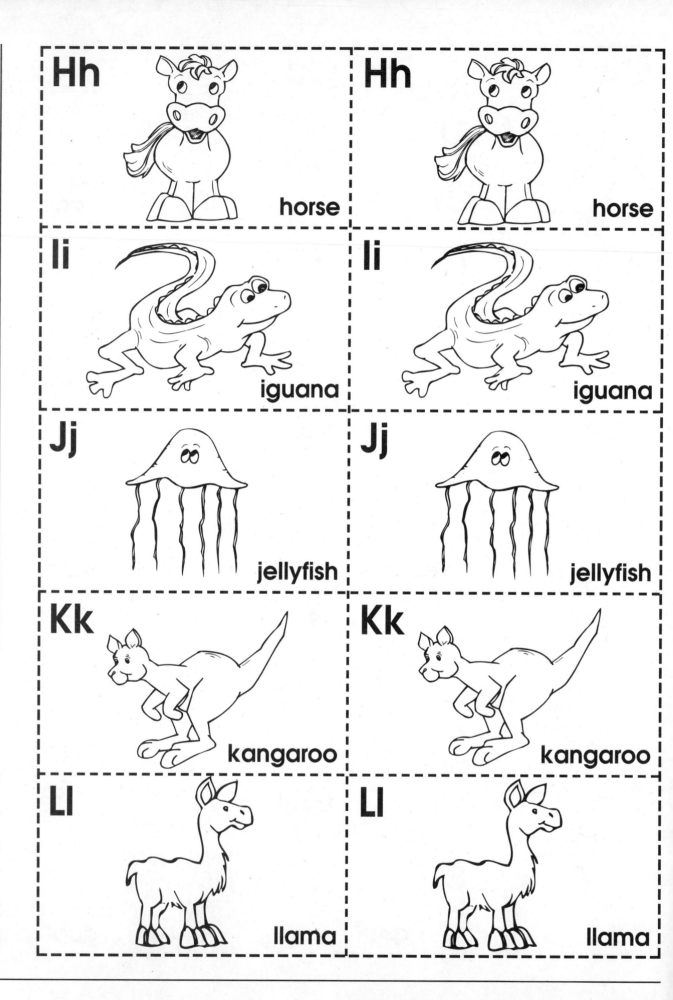

Hh horse

Hh horse

Ii iguana

Ii iguana

Jj jellyfish

Jj jellyfish

Kk kangaroo

Kk kangaroo

Ll llama

Ll llama

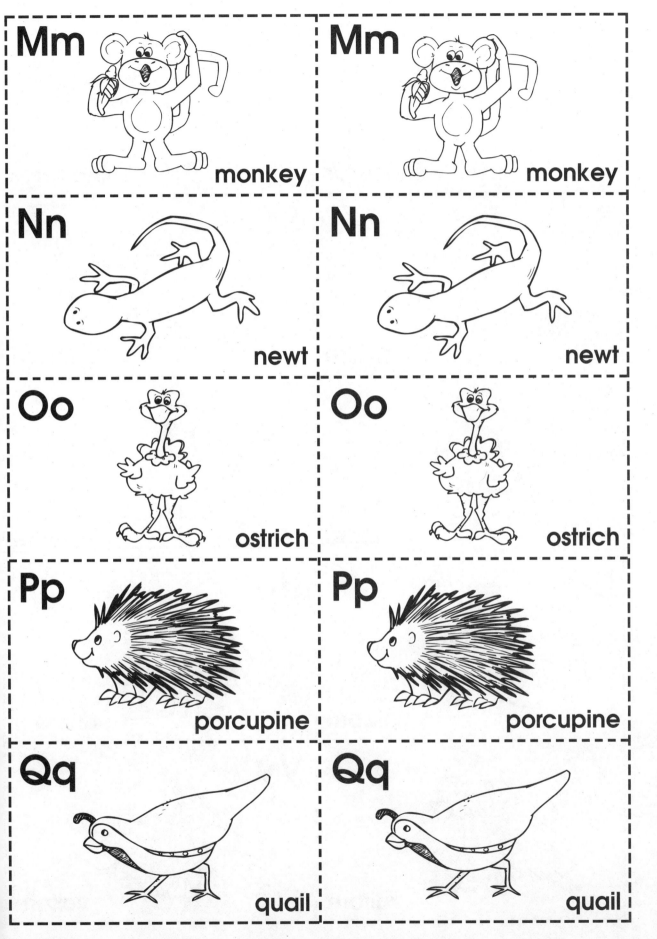

**Mm** monkey

**Mm** monkey

**Nn** newt

**Nn** newt

**Oo** ostrich

**Oo** ostrich

**Pp** porcupine

**Pp** porcupine

**Qq** quail

**Qq** quail

**Zz**

**Game**

Z

**Rr** rhinoceros

**Rr** rhinoceros

**Ss** snake

**Ss** snake

**Tt** turtle

**Tt** turtle

**Uu** unicorn

**Uu** unicorn

**Vv** vulture

**Vv** vulture

**Ww** walrus

**Ww** walrus

**Xx** xenopus

**Xx** xenopus

**Yy** yak

**Yy** yak

**Zz** zebra

**Zz** zebra

**Wild Card**

**Wild Card**

**Z**

# Z Is for Zucchini

**A**lthough zucchini is a very versatile and delicious food, you may find that many of your students have never tasted it.

## Zucchini Sticks and Dip
### United States

Zucchini is a great vegetable to dip.
1. Use serrated, plastic knives to peel the zucchini and cut into sticks.
2. Dip in onion dip, sour cream, ranch dressing, mayonnaise or any other favorite dip.

## Stuffed Zucchini
### The Middle East

1. Wash zucchini and cut off the stem. Using an apple corer, scoop out the pulp taking care not to break the skin. One end should remain closed. Save pulp.
2. To make the filling for each zucchini, you will need 2 tablespoons (30 ml) pizza or spaghetti sauce and 2 tablespoons (30 ml) chopped zucchini pulp. Mix filling in a bowl and then stuff it in the zucchini.
3. Layer the stuffed zucchini in a pan. Cover with stewed tomatoes or spaghetti sauce. Put a lid on the pan and cook over very low heat for 1 hour or until the zucchini is tender.

## French Fried Zucchini
### France

1. Let the children wash, peel and cut the zucchini into 1/2" (1.25 cm) thick rings.
2. Dip in seasoning salt and flour.
3. Use an electric skillet to fry the rings. Use cooking tongs to remove zucchini from hot grease. Place on paper towels to drain. Serve warm.

# ZENITH!

_____

knows the shapes of the uppercase and lowercase **Z**.

## Amazzzzzzing!

You know the sounds the letter **Z** makes.

**To:** _____

# Excellent!

_____

knows the letters from A to Z!

## Zeeee Award

**for Zeee Best!**

To: _____

## Dear Parents,

**S**oon our class will be studying the uppercase and lowercase letter **A**. We will be learning the attached nursery rhymes. If you have the opportunity, please recite them with your child. We will be playing a foods game to introduce the sound of each letter of the alphabet. At family mealtimes, talk about the beginning letter of one or two of the foods you are eating. We will be making books with animals that begin with **A** including armadillo, ant, anteater, ape and alligator; and we will be sculpting uppercase and lowercase **A**s with bread dough and cookie dough. We will celebrate **A** by preparing different apple dishes. If you can prepare or help the children prepare an apple dish in class, please let me know, and a copy of the recipes will be sent home to you.

**I**f you have any of the following that you can donate to the class for our craft or food projects, please send them to school with your child: apples, lemon, acorns, loaf of bread, apple jelly, apple butter, frozen ready-made cookie or bread dough, spice cake mix and frozen ready-made pastry shells.

## Dear Parents,

**S**oon our class will study the uppercase and lowercase letter **B**. We will learn the attached nursery rhymes. If you have the opportunity, please practice them with your child. We will play a game to learn the children's full names. Activities focus on foods that begin with **B** including: bacon, bagels, bananas, beans, bread, broccoli, blueberries, butter, Brussels sprouts, biscuits, brownies and butterscotch candy. We will be playing **B** picture card rummy and the colors blue, brown and black will be introduced, too. To celebrate **B** we will be making a banana dessert. If you can prepare or help the children prepare a banana dish in class, please let me know, and a copy of the recipes will be sent home with your child.

**I**f you have any of the following that you can donate to the class for our craft or food projects, please send them to school with your child: beans, beads, large buttons, bananas, can of coconut milk and one lemon or lime.

## Dear Parents,

We will be studying the uppercase and lowercase letter **C** soon. We will be learning the attached nursery rhymes. Ask your child to share one of the rhymes with you. The soft sound of **C** (S) and the hard sound of **C** (K) will be introduced using pictures of these foods: carrots, cauliflower, cantaloupes, corn, cucumbers, cabbage, cider, cereal and celery. When your family eats a food that begins with **C**, identify it as a hard **C** or soft **C** sound. To celebrate **C** we will making a cake or candy recipe. If you can prepare or help the children prepare a cake or candy dish in class, please let me know, and a copy of the recipes will be sent home to you.

If you have any of the following that you can donate to the class for our craft projects or snacks, please send them to school with your child: animal crackers, candy corn, hard candies, coconut, round cookies, box of instant chocolate pudding, two eggs, Ricotta cheese, oranges, pint of whipping cream, chocolate chips, peanuts and raisins.

## Dear Parents,

Soon our class will study the uppercase and lowercase letter **D**. We will learn the attached nursery rhymes. If you have the opportunity, please practice the **D** rhymes with your child. We will be doing several projects and playing picture dominoes with animals that begin with **D**, including: duck, donkey, dog, dinosaur, dolphin, dragon and deer. We will learn a finger play for "Dance, Thumbkin." Ask your child to share that with you. We will be making paper plate clocks to reinforce "Dickery, Dickery, Dock" and eating dumplings for "Deedle, Deedle, Dumpling, My Son John." If you can prepare or help the children prepare dumplings in class, please let me know, and a copy of the recipes will be sent to you.

If you have any of the following that you can donate to the class for our craft projects or snacks, please send them to school with your child: paper plates, apples, mixed dried fruit, a lemon, brown sugar and eggs.

**Ee**

## Dear Parents,

Our class will be studying the uppercase and lowercase letter **E**. We will be reciting the attached nursery rhymes. Please use these rhymes with your child. Example: "Early to bed and early to rise" can be recited when tucking your child in bed. "Eggs, butter, cheese, bread" can be used when sending your child off to do a task. We will be using echo games to learn the rhymes, which may be yet another way of sharing the rhymes with your child. We will be discussing our ears and eyes. We will create **E** creatures and an E.L. Ephant autograph craft. Egg recipes are planned for our foods project. If you can prepare or help the children prepare an egg dish in class, please let me know, and a copy of the recipes will be sent home to you.

If you have any of the following that you can donate to the class, for our craft or food projects, please send them to school with your child: egg cartons, crushed eggshells, large movable craft eyes, hard-boiled eggs, ready-made pastry shells, paper baking cups or cheddar cheese.

**Ff**

## Dear Parents,

Soon our class will be studying the uppercase and lowercase letter **F**. We will learn the attached nursery rhymes. If you have the opportunity, please practice the **F** rhymes with your child. We will practice counting to ten, make fingerprint pictures and create personal flags. We will be doing several projects based on animals that begin with **F**, including: fly, firefly, fox, fawn, fish and frog. To celebrate the letter **F**, we will have a fruit festival. If you can prepare or help children prepare a fruit recipe in class, please let me know, and a copy of the recipes will be sent home with your child.

If you have any of the following that you can donate to the class for our craft or food projects, please send them to school with your child: feathers, fake fur, fuzz (dryer lint), old magazines, a bag of frozen berries. Every child will be asked to bring to class one piece of his very favorite fruit for a salad. I will let you know which day.

## Dear Parents,

We will be studying the uppercase and lowercase letter **G**. We will be learning the attached nursery rhymes. If you have the opportunity, please practice them with your child. We will be sewing little pillows of animals that begin with **G** and drawing giant **G**s on the playground. Ginger goodies will be made and served to culminate our **G** unit. If you can prepare or help the children prepare a ginger dish in class, please let me know, and a copy of the recipes will be sent home to you.

If you have any of the following that you can donate to the class for our craft or food projects, please send them to school with your child: green, gold, and gray (silver) glitter; gingersnaps; peanut butter; box of ginger-bread mix; pint of whipping cream; graham crackers; can of vanilla icing; raisins; dried fruit; candy decorations.

## Dear Parents,

Soon our class will study the uppercase and lowercase letter **H**. We will learn the attached nursery rhymes. Ask your child to recite some of the rhymes to you. We will discuss our hands and create handkerchief dolls. Each child will need two large, white handkerchiefs. (Mark initials in one corner.) The concepts of one-half and harmony will be introduced. For a treat, we will be making hoagies and honey butter. If you can prepare or help the children prepare hoagies in class, please let me know, and a copy of the recipes will be sent home to you.

If you have any of the following that you can donate to the class for our craft or food projects, please send them to school with your child: felt pieces, large white handkerchiefs, mayonnaise, mustard, American cheese, Swiss cheese, other cheeses, various lunch meats, tomatoes, lettuce, French bread, honey and butter.

## Dear Parents,

**S**oon our class will be studying the uppercase and lowercase letter **I**. We will be learning the attached nursery rhymes. Practice them with your child. We will be learning to sing a round in two parts, so you may want to sing the rhymes as a round with your child. We will also be making a life-sized paper doll of each student, discussing the things that make us happy and sharing what makes each one of us unique. Talk to your child about the things that make her special to you. We will be playing a game called If . . . . Ask her to teach you the game; it is something families can do on long trips in the car. Ice-cream dishes will be served to culminate the **I** unit. If you can prepare or help the children prepare an ice-cream dish in class, please let me know, and a copy of the recipes will be sent home to you.

**I**f you have any of the following that you can donate to the class for our craft or food projects, please send them to school with your child: old shirts or jeans the children can cut up and attach to their life-sized paper dolls; sheets of 8" x 8" (20.32 x 20.32 cm) felt; beads; buttons; blunt, plastic needles; yarn; thread; white glitter; waxed paper; ice cream and your child's favorite ice-cream topping.

## Dear Parents,

**O**ur class will be studying the uppercase and lowercase letter **J**. We will learning the attached nursery rhymes and using them to jump rope. Take time to jump rope with your child. We will be discussing jazz music and singing the rhymes in a "jazzy" way. We will be using "junk" (recycled materials) to create a treasure. Discuss the importantce of recycling with your youngster. To celebrate **J** we will be making and sampling jam and jelly. If you can prepare or help the children make jam or jelly in class, please let me know, and a copy of the recipes will be sent home to you.

**I**f you have any of the following that you can donate to the class for our craft or food projects, please send them to school with your child: old magazines, thin elastic for stringing paper beads, flavored instant coffee tins, large grocery bags, oatmeal cartons, rickrack, sequins, glitter, paper plates, frozen or fresh strawberries, grape juice concentrate, ready-made sugar cookie dough, aluminum foil, a box of pectin, jelly jars and lids.

# Dear Parents,

**S**oon our class will be studying the uppercase and lowercase letter **K**. We will be learning the attached nursery rhymes. If you have the opportunity, please practice them with your child. We will practice tying knots. The sound of hard **K** and silent **K** will be introduced. Students will make picture flash cards for these words that begin with **K**: ketchup, King Cole, kitten, kite, koala, key, kangaroo and kitchen. To culminate our **K** unit, children will be constructing and tasting kebabs. If you can prepare a kebab dish to bring to class, please let me know, and a copy of the recipes will be sent to you.

**I**f you have any of the following that you can donate to the class for our craft or food projects, please send them to school with your child: new household sponges, paper plates, party toothpicks, American cheese, Swiss cheese, cheddar cheese, ham, salami, shrimp, cauliflower, carrots, celery, green peppers, cherry tomatoes, apples, bananas, pineapple, cherries, grapes and any other foods that can be skewed on picks.

# Dear Parents,

**S**oon our class will be studying the uppercase and lowercase letter **L**. We will be learning the attached nursery rhymes and creating new lyrics for each. As a home game, change words slightly in rhymes and make up new lyrics for them. We will be making paper links, creating **L** stories and sorting **L** objects into appropriate sets. Children will also be playing a concentration card game with **L** pictures. We will have a luscious **L** lunch to culminate this unit. If you can prepare or help the children prepare an **L** recipe in class, please let me know, and a copy of the recipes will be sent home to you.

**I**f you have any of the following that you can donate to the class for our craft projects or snacks, please send them to school with your child: rick-rack, ribbon, lima beans, lentils, ham bone, lettuce, cream cheese, chicken breasts, minced garlic, onion, green pepper, tomatoes, lime, chicken broth, tortilla chips, ready-made cookie dough and lemon icing.

## Dear Parents,

**S**oon our class will be studying the uppercase and lowercase letter **M**. We will be learning the two attached nursery rhymes. If you have the opportunity, please practice them with your child. We will be introducing the concepts: mosaics, murals, mimicking and mazes. We will also be creating **M** animal masks and wearing them to play **M** games. We plan to mold marzipan for a snack one day. If you can prepare or help the children prepare marzipan in class, please let me know, and a copy of the recipes will be sent home to you.

**I**f you have any of the following that you can donate to the class for our craft or food projects, please send them to school with your child: macaroni, large heavy paper plates, craft sticks, almond paste, confectioners' sugar, eggs, white corn syrup, almond extract, coconut flakes, box of flavored gelatin and sweetened condensed milk.

## Dear Parents,

**S**oon we will be studying the uppercase and lowercase letter **N**. We will be learning the attached nursery rhymes. If you have the opportunity, please practice them with your child. We will be focusing on our noses, making papier-mâché **N**s, and rewriting an **N** rhyme. We will eat noodles to culminate this unit. If you can prepare or help the children prepare a noodle dish in class, please let me know, and a copy of the recipes will be sent home to you.

**I**f you have any of the following that you can donate to the class for our craft or food projects, please send them to school with your child: old newspapers, wide egg noodles, vermicelli noodles, can of chicken broth, soy sauce, one 12 oz. (340.2 kg) green spinach noodles, tomato sauce, Parmesan cheese, ramen noodles (Chinese style), sesame seeds and peanuts.

## Dear Parents,

**O**ur class will be studying the uppercase and lowercase letter **O** soon. We will be learning the attached nursery rhymes. If you have the opportunity, recite the rhymes with your child. This unit focuses on music. We will be singing the rhymes as an opera, learning the song "Old MacDonald Had a Farm" and making musical instruments. Children will create their own rebus story of "Old Mother Hubbard" and match some **O** animal words and pictures. We will prepare and eat some round foods that begin with **O**. If you can prepare or help the children prepare a round **O** dish in class, please let me know, and a copy of the recipes will be sent home to you.

**I**f you have any of the following that you can donate to the class for our craft or food projects, please send them to school with your child: O-shaped cereal or pasta, old magazines, coffee cans, throwaway pie tins, bolts, nuts, tissue boxes, tissue rolls, rice, beans, macaroni, clay pots, all sizes of rubber bands, pancake mix, onions, oranges, English muffins, pizza sauce, cheese and black olives.

## Dear Parents,

**S**oon our class will be studying the uppercase and lowercase letter **P**. We will be learning the attached nursery rhymes. If you have the opportunity, please practice them with your child. We will be learning what pease porridge is and doing activities that teach the concepts of *hot* and *cold*. Children will construct puppets, practice tongue twisters and make pink pudding paint. Peanuts and peanut butter will be our food focus. If you can prepare or help the children prepare a peanut dish in class, please let me know, and a copy of the recipes will be sent home to you.

**I**f you have any of the following that you can donate to the class for our craft or food projects, please send them to school with your child: split peas, old socks, beads, large felt squares, feathers, red and pink felt scraps, peanuts in shells, lunch sacks, newspapers, cotton balls, toothpicks, plastic spoons, pipe cleaners, cloth scraps, vegetables, fruits, raisins, paper plates, instant vanilla pudding, milk, instant strawberry pudding, raw peanuts, chicken broth, milk, peanut butter, dry milk powder, honey, wheat germ, jelly, crispy rice cereal, chocolate chips, chopped peanuts, a loaf of white bread and a loaf of wheat bread.

## Dear Parents,

**S**oon our class will study the uppercase and lowercase letter **Q**. We will learn the two attached nursery rhymes. We will discuss queens and kings. We will also construct a large paper quilt. If you have a quilt that you can share with the class, please bring it. We will spend some time learning about being quiet and practice some relaxation techniques. We will prepare and sample tarts to celebrate the Queen of Hearts. If you can prepare or help children prepare tarts in class, please let me know, and a copy of the recipes will be sent home to you.

**I**f you have any of the following that you can donate to the class for our craft or food projects, please send them to school with your child: glitter, sequins, ribbons, roll of aluminum foil, gold foil wrapping paper, gummed stars, stickers, old magazines, Q-tips™, dried yeast, milk, flour, lemon, butter, ripe plums, ready-made pastry shell and eggs.

**Rr**

> ## Dear Parents,
>
> Soon our class will be studying the uppercase and lowercase letter **R**. We will be learning the attached nursery rhymes. When reciting rhymes with your child, ask her what she did in class with the rhyme. We will be discussing the weather, especially rain and rainbows. Children will be asked to solve rhyming riddles. We will make raspberry dishes to celebrate our work with **R**. If you can prepare or help the children prepare a raspberry recipe in class, please let me know, and a copy of the recipes will be sent home to you.
>
> If you have any of the following that you can donate to the class for our craft or food projects, please send them to school with your child: paper cups, rice, food coloring, tissue paper, pipe cleaners, ready-made sugar cookie dough, raspberry jam, flour, heavy cream, butter, frozen raspberries or fresh raspberries and vanilla ice cream.

**Ss**

> ## Dear Parents,
>
> Soon our class will be studying the uppercase and lowercase letter **S**. We will be learning the attached nursery rhymes. If you have the opportunity, say or sing them with your child. The activities in this unit will focus on the seashore and animals that swim. Sounds that begin with **S** (snore, snap, sniff) will be used to play a game. Students will write squiggle stories and make **S** word picture flash cards. We will sample chicken pie and make strawberry shortcake. If you can prepare or help the children prepare a dish in class to culminate the **S** unit, please let me know, and a copy of the recipes will be sent home to you.
>
> If you have any of the following that you can donate to the class for our craft or food projects, please send them to school with your child: silk scraps, stones, seashells, sand, ready-made pastry shells, cooked chicken breasts, mushrooms, carrots, potatoes, heavy cream, shortcake, frozen or fresh strawberries.

**Tt**

> ## Dear Parents,
>
> Soon our class will be studying the uppercase and lowercase letter **T**. We will be learning the attached nursery rhymes. If you have the opportunity, please practice them with your child. We will be discussing the stars and singing Mozart's first song "Twinkle, Twinkle, Little Star." Take the opportunity to star gaze with your child. She may want to sing "Twinkle, Twinkle, Little Star" under the night sky. In crafts we will be tearing **T**s to make tapestries and creating a "Tom, Tom, the Piper's Son" book. A tea party will culminate our unit. If you would like to attend our tea party, please note that you are welcome.
>
> If you have any of the following that you can donate to the class for our craft or food projects, please send them to school with your child: large, gummed silver stars; old magazines; fruity and mint herb tea bags; green tea; instant rice; sugar; honey; cream and lemons.